T0311914

Educating the Covid Generation

The Covid pandemic has caused massive disruption in the education system. The consequences for the education of the next generation are now clearly visible: a decline in learning performance, problems in psycho-social development, and a deterioration in physical condition. Although all children and young people are affected, those from educationally deprived backgrounds fall behind the most. All this characterizes the Covid Generation. Educational inequity is on the rise, and an educational catastrophe is looming.

As important as this look back is, it is crucial to look forward. This vital book addresses the future of the Covid Generation by exploring its central issues, such as:

- What must be done to educate the Covid Generation in the best possible way?
- What concepts are there from an educational science perspective?
- What are the lessons learned from the Covid pandemic that will continue to be important for the education system in the future?
- What new teaching and learning structures need to be created?
- How can we strengthen student and teacher resilience?

Based on an empirical survey of the well-being and educational attainment of the Covid Generation, concepts and ideas are presented to support and develop the Covid Generation of students, to rethink the education system, and to overcome the educational climate crisis and to enable a fresh start.

Klaus Zierer is Professor of Education at the University of Augsburg, Germany, and Associate Research Fellow of the Centre on Skills, Knowledge and Organisational Performance at the University of Oxford, UK. He co-authored the bestselling *10 Mindframes for Visible Learning* and *Visible Learning Insights* with John Hattie.

Educating the Covid Generation
How We Can Prevent the Impending
Educational Catastrophe after Covid

Klaus Zierer

Routledge
Taylor & Francis Group

LONDON AND NEW YORK

First edition published 2023
by Routledge
4 Park Square, Milton Park, Abingdon, Oxon, OX14 4RN

and by Routledge
605 Third Avenue, New York, NY 10158

Routledge is an imprint of the Taylor & Francis Group, an informa business

British Library Cataloguing-in-Publication Data
A catalogue record for this book is available from the British Library

ISBN: 978-1-032-52874-8 (hbk)
ISBN: 978-1-032-52873-1 (pbk)
ISBN: 978-1-003-40886-4 (ebk)

DOI: 10.4324/9781003408864

Typeset in Times New Roman
by SPi Technologies India Pvt Ltd (Straive)

Contents

Foreword

I have written this book primarily from the perspective of a professor of school education, but also as a former teacher and father of three children. The Covid-19 pandemic has changed many things in society as a whole and has challenged families in particular. More than ever before, they have become the centre of education.

What I myself have experienced in recent months has spurred me on again and again to take a stand in the daily press and to get involved in shaping public opinion.

Although there was a lot of discussion about the measures to contain Covid, in my opinion, it was not from the perspective of children and young people. To this day, I consider them to be the part of society that is not heard enough. The lip service repeatedly paid to them by politicians does not change that.

When I look at my three children – Quirin is in the third grade, Zacharias in the sixth grade, and Viktoria in the eighth grade – it fills me with concern that they have spent more time at home than at school between 2020 and 2022. How is a young person supposed to develop if they are cut off from the outside world, isolated from friends, quarantined again and again, and not allowed to do all the things that make life worth living? Learning at home is a challenge and cannot replace school. It lacks the power of peers, indeed the power of teachers and the power of school. It lacks the strength of our peers, the strength of the teachers, and the strength of the school.

We have not fallen as a family, but we have stumbled many times. The Covid-19 pandemic shook the family structure again and again. In these moments, I imagined how it must be for families who do not have the same conditions as we do: families who have no previous educational experience, who do not have a secure income, where both parents have to work, who live in the narrow city and not in the wide countryside, who have to fight for their existence every day and who have care cases in their immediate environment. The climate of concern must be many times greater in these families and must, in the worst case, become a climate of fear. Those who do not succeed in this change of perspective or, worse, who are left cold by it, should not enter politics. After all, the related question of educational justice is one of the core questions of democracy. If it falls victim to political banter, democracy is also threatened. All children and young people have a right to the best possible education. One is not born an educational loser; one is made an educational loser. No human being should be left behind.

To this day, the education system has not managed to offer solutions on how to implement this political maxim. It has not been idle, and a lot of money has been put into the education system. But as is so often the case, the measures financed with it were not thought through to the end, so that much quickly fizzled out. Often, they addressed problems only at the surface, but not in depth. The digital upgrading of children's rooms with tablets is one such example: this is neither a guarantee for educational success nor should it happen without pedagogical support. I am deliberately talking about the education system, because it is not just about educational policy, not just about schools, not just about teachers. Education is a task for society as a whole, and all citizens of a country bear responsibility for the next generation.

Thus, the collateral damage of the measures taken to contain the Covid-19 pandemic is clearly visible today and is hitting children and young people particularly hard. Without a doubt, learning performance has declined. Likewise, children's physical condition has been damaged, and their psycho-social development has also suffered. The health of children and young people has been tarnished, as has their education. We have to recognise that children and young people are the ones to suffer from the crisis. The problems mentioned will not be easy to solve. They will challenge us for years to come.

The Covid-19 pandemic has shaken the education system and at the same time exposed known weaknesses in a dramatic way. We are stumbling through this crisis from an educational policy perspective and are not managing to give children and young people an educational perspective. It is hard to avoid the impression that educational policy is turning a blind eye to this – both to the collateral damage and to the known weak points. The responsibility of the older generation for the younger generation forbids us to look the other way. It is time for a wake-up call.

The education of children and young people is not only a country's most important resource. It is the most valuable thing a society produces. Children and young people do not belong to us. Rather, we hand over to them this one world as we inherited it from our mothers and fathers and shaped it mostly to the best of our knowledge and conscience. So it is our responsibility how we lead children and young people into this one world. We need a climate of trust and confidence, a climate of security and joy, a climate in which the human being consists not only of a head but also of a body and a soul, a climate in which cognitive performance, as important as it is, does not stand above all other dimensions of the human being. We need a climate in which social togetherness is important, in which the human being with all his or her possibilities is given a place, is listened to, and is supported by all the forces at our disposal.

This book was written against this background. It was written above all for all children and young people and their families who have felt in the Covid-19 pandemic that the education system is faltering and lagging behind the times. Likewise, it is addressed to all those who have educational policy responsibility or are part of the education system. Perhaps it will succeed in conveying the learners' perspective. For it is only from their eyes that an education system can be meaningfully reformed. And so this book is also written for the following generations to have an education system that has learned from the Covid-19 pandemic and supports all children and young people in the best possible way.

I am pleased to say that I received many letters in response to my articles in the daily press, not only a few critical voices, which are always welcome, but above all a lot of approval. These encouraged me to start working on this book and I would like to thank Bruce Roberts of Routledge for his assistance in publishing it. It first appeared in German under the title *Ein Jahr zum Vergessen* [A Year to Forget] by Herder in 2021. The ambiguity is what spoke most to many people: a year to forget, because children and young people, parents and also teachers would like to leave the last year behind and not be reminded of it. Many situations were too difficult, too challenging, too stressful. And also a year to forget with regard to education. Children and young people have forgotten many things. Learning deficits are clearly visible, physical deficits cannot be covered up, and social development has also been damaged by the measures taken to contain the Covid-19 pandemic.

If I look back now, in the year 2023, not much has really happened in the field of education. The problems we already saw in 2021 are becoming increasingly clear. We must face the facts and learn from the Covid-19 pandemic. The next generation is a special generation. It is the Covid Generation. Educating them is not only our challenge but also our responsibility. The time is ripe for an educational climate change. As apt as the exaggeration of the title is, I do not want to stop at the level of alarmism and powerlessness. Rather, my concern is to look forward. As a school educator, I am firmly convinced that we humans can accomplish a lot and achieve a lot. If, indeed, we succeed in joining forces, basing our power of judgement on reason, sharpening it through joint dialogue, and transforming a thirst for action into creative power, then we still have the opportunity to avert and prevent an impending educational catastrophe. There is not much time left. But with determination, we can all succeed.

This book aims to contribute to this by opening up perspectives for a school of the future in addition to diagnosing the current situation. Rethinking schools and thus also rethinking education is the order of the day. All readers are invited to critically and constructively engage with my reflections so that together we can develop a sustainable vision of education for our children and young people.

Marklkofen, January 2023
Klaus Zierer

1   The Covid-19 pandemic and its measures from an educational perspective

For some time now, the Covid-19 pandemic has kept the world on tenterhooks. The measures taken do not always work as hoped and entail collateral damage that should not go unnoticed. For all the urgency to protect people's health, health includes not only physical integrity but also psychological and social components, and all three are interdependent. A person who is physically healthy, for example, can nevertheless be ill if he or she has psychological ailments or is socially isolated – and the reverse is of course equally true. It is not uncommon for a symptom of illness in one of these areas to lead to damage to the person's overall health: a mental disorder can follow from a physical disability, physical impairments can emerge from a mental burden, and so on. In a figurative sense, this concept of health also applies to systems such as the family, the economy, or schools.

If we look at schools, there are increasing indications that an educational catastrophe is looming and that children and young people from educationally disadvantaged backgrounds are particularly affected. There is no doubt that the educational gap has always been considerable – especially in some Western countries like Germany – and this has not least to do with the diversity of cultural imprints in families. Educational inequalities are thus part of the core business of education. But the school-based measures taken to curb the Covid-19 pandemic have exacerbated this situation and continue to do so. Educational inequity is thus massively increasing. An educational catastrophe is looming.

Now it would be wrong to accuse educational policy of having done nothing. On the contrary, a lot has been done and a lot of money has been spent. But as is so often the case, it must be recognised: educational success does not come about simply because the education system receives a financial injection. Moreover, not every well-intentioned measure leads to success – especially if it has not been thought through to the end and the stakeholders concerned are not adequately involved. These are first and foremost the learners, the teachers, and the parents. Education is one of the most important tasks of a society because it is the guarantor of

DOI: 10.4324/9781003408864-1

economic, ecological, and social prosperity. And education is also a complex matter and demands the participation of all those involved.

Many are put off by the very attempt to define the concept of education. This is not good for the discourse, because clarity in terms goes hand
in hand with clarity in thought and clarity in action. Without a clearly
outlined leitmotif, no educational policy can be pursued. In this respect, it
is essential to outline the concept of education and, building on this, to
address the previously mentioned concepts of educational inequality and
educational justice. Both are political fighting words today and are repeatedly brought up in elections. Despite their almost self-evident use in everyday life, they are not easy to understand either: what are inequalities?
What is justice? And how can they be understood in connection with the
concept of education? This is also not the first time there has been talk of
an educational catastrophe; I will trace the debate on this term that has
already taken place in the past, especially in Germany. This historical ret-
rospective is helpful, indeed necessary, if we wish to better understand the
present and formulate coherent concepts for the future.

There are three sub-aspects that are illuminated in the following, laying
the foundation for this book: first, an outline of the measures in the educational field that were taken to contain the Covid-19 pandemic; second,
a review of the educational catastrophe in the 1960s; and third, a clarification of the terms 'education', 'educational inequalities', and 'educational
justice'.

School closures: an educational disaster?

When a new form of pneumonia was confirmed in Wuhan, China, on 31
December 2019, there was global media coverage, but further policy action was not yet taken. It was only when this disease, named 'Covid-19',
became an epidemic in China and quickly spread around the world that
all countries responded to the situation. From then on, the so-called
Covid-19 pandemic was dominant in all regions and in all areas of life.

In addition to keeping one's distance, observing hygiene, and wearing a
mask in everyday life, known as 'hands – face – space – rules', lockdown
measures were repeatedly implemented in many countries from March
2020 on, largely shutting down public life. Schools were also affected and
closed for extended periods of time – some for several weeks (e.g., Switzerland), some for several months to a year (e.g., Germany), and some for
over a year (e.g., Bangladesh). The aim of the measures was obvious: lim-
iting social contacts in order to contain the spread of the virus. Distance
learning was offered where possible in the interest of still fulfilling the educational mandate. The term 'homeschooling' quickly became established
in the German media in this context. Even though this term is misleading,
because homeschooling in the form of lessons organised privately at home

is not allowed in some countries, it clearly captures the core of the problem: the boundaries between the family system and the school system became blurred, causing great challenges in many places. Thus, some families saw themselves well equipped to support their children in learning, while others failed to do so. That educationally disadvantaged milieus and socially disadvantaged families in particular have a harder time is obvious in view of the numerous studies on educational inequalities.

Between the years 2020 and 2022, school closures were the method of choice above a certain incidence rate. They were accompanied by a digitalisation push that focused on equipping schools and upgrading children's rooms. In Germany, for example, on top of the five billion euros of the so-called digital pact for schools (DigitalPakt Schule) from 2018, which has not been fully drawn down to date, the federal government made an additional 500 million euros available in the summer of 2020 to equip learners with tablets. The same amount was added again to provide teachers with a service device. Many German states added even more. In addition, masks were purchased, spit shields erected, guidance systems recorded, and in some cases room filters and ventilation systems installed. In addition to face-to-face teaching and distance teaching, another form of schooling practised was a hybrid teaching format in which the class is halved and thus fewer children are in school at the same time. Graduating classes generally entered schools faster than others. These measures were linked to the hope in educational policy that enough had been done to ensure educational success even in pandemic times – for all learners.

If you add up the times when children and young people were not in school, it quickly amounts to several weeks, in some cases even months or years. Depending on the age of the learners, the country, and the incidence rates, some learners can look back on more time spent at home than at school in the years between 2020 and 2022. In this respect, two school years have already been massively affected by the Covid-19 pandemic in this generation. Educational policy long ignored the fact that all this will not remain without consequences in the long run. Later, the approach was to pay lip service, as in Germany: after the first school closures in spring 2020, it was said everywhere that children should not be the ones to suffer again and that schools should remain open. Reality quickly caught up with this talk. While industry continued to produce and professional football rolled on, children and young people had to learn alone in front of the screens again. To this day, it is astonishing to hear the statements made by some presidents or ministers that everything was working fine.

Meanwhile, one only has to look into educationally deprived milieus, visit socially disadvantaged families, or talk to children and young people. They are suffering from the situation. Moreover, there are more and more studies showing the extent of the drama. Not only has learning performance declined, but there has also been an increase in mental and psychosomatic illnesses as well as physical impairments. The mental, physical, and social health of children and young people is affected.

Just as in the medical battle against the Covid-19 pandemic, it is therefore high time to finally listen to science in the educational field as well. But there is not too much time left. The education catastrophe is in full swing.

Perhaps one might object that it is alarmist to speak of an educational catastrophe. After all, things are not that bad. Two things must be said to the contrary: on the one hand, the full extent of the educational catastrophe must be empirically proven, which is the topic of the second chapter of this book. Second, it should be noted that the term 'educational catastrophe' already has a history, e. g. in Germany, and served as the driving force behind a debate whose initial situation was certainly threatening. But compared to the current situation, it seems harmless because the abuses of that time are not even remotely comparable to those on display today. Not for nothing, for example, did the German federal government announce in the spring of 2021 that it would provide one billion euros for a tutoring programme. Awareness of the problems seems to be growing clearer by the day. But the tutoring programme has failed. Money alone does not close gaps in education, it does not cure social loneliness, and it does not give back exercise time. A fundamental change in the educational climate is necessary.

The education catastrophe of the 1960s – and the lessons learnt

The 1960s saw major changes in the education system in some countries around the world. The developments in Germany can be used as an example to outline these changes and to draw important conclusions for the current debate about a possible education catastrophe.

It was first and foremost the educator, philosopher, and theologian Georg Picht (1913–1982) who introduced the term 'educational catastrophe'. The starting point was a series of articles in the German weekly newspaper *Christ und Welt* [Christ and World] in 1964, which at the time was one of the highest-circulation and most influential print media in the still young Federal Republic of Germany. In his articles, Georg Picht analysed the German education system with the help of extensive data. His diagnosis was clear: Germany was facing an educational catastrophe that would lead to serious disadvantages in international comparison and could even endanger democracy.

Georg Picht saw the reasons for the educational catastrophe in at least the following four points: first, he noted a shortage of teachers, which would lead to greater disadvantages in the long run. Second, he criticised the fact that there were too few high school graduates. Third, he called for an unfair distribution of educational opportunities. And fourth, he criticised design flaws in the control and administration of the education system, which exacerbated all the aforementioned points.

Georg Picht formulated an emergency programme against this educational emergency. In it, he drew up proposals for organising the education system, modernising the rural school system, doubling the number of school leavers, increasing the number of teachers at grammar schools and also at primary schools, and reorganising the administration of education. His conclusion at the time was: "Every nation has the education system it deserves. It is still possible to prevent the full force of the educational catastrophe from befalling us. Germany can still be preserved as a cultural state. But this requires a decisive turnaround".

Georg Picht was not alone in this description of the state of the German education system. A number of well-known people of the time supported his thoughts. First and foremost, Ralf Dahrendorf, who was not only one of the leading sociologists in the 1960s but was also able to exert greater political influence through his political activities for the liberal-democratic party. In his work *Bildung ist Bürgerrecht* [Education is a civil right], he supported Picht's position and also coined the well-known formula for disadvantages in the education system at that time: the Catholic working-class girl from the countryside, comparable today perhaps to the boy with a migration background from the big city. The discussions initiated by Georg Picht and Ralf Dahrendorf had a far-reaching influence on the educational policy of the time. Two measures that can be associated with them should be mentioned in the present context.

First, the German Education Council was set up by the federal and state governments in 1965 to draw up needs and development plans for the German education system. These plans served as the basis for structural proposals and recommendations for long-term planning. The "Structural Plan for Education" presented in 1970 was particularly influential, and its impact is still felt to this day. With the exception of the universities, almost all areas of the education system were taken into consideration. From today's perspective, this publication is a testimony to the spirit of optimism in educational policy that prevailed after the student unrest of 1968 and as a result of the social-liberal coalition from 1969 onwards.

Second, the Federal-State Commission for Educational Planning and Research Promotion was convened in 1970. Until the end of 2007, it was the permanent forum for discussion on questions of education and research funding that concerned both the federation and the states. The commission made recommendations on education planning and research funding at both the federal and state levels.

Even though there was great euphoria at first and some changes took place, the reforms in the education sector came to a halt sooner than many had thought they would. With increasing distance, there were also more and more voices saying that some reforms missed the target of averting an educational catastrophe, and even the diagnosis of Georg Picht and Ralf Dahrendorf is not shared unreservedly today.

If one nevertheless tries to draw conclusions from the debate about the German education system of that time that are still relevant today, three points become apparent: first, it is important for each generation to reconsider for itself what education means and what value it has. In doing so, it is not enough to consider only structural issues of the education system – probably one of the major weaknesses of the debate about an educational disaster from the 1960s. Second, it is indisputable that not all people have the same prerequisites for education, but that everyone nevertheless has a right to education. In this context, such educational inequalities are not only the responsibility of the individual but in a democracy always the responsibility of all. As before, this issue is so central that it can only be overlooked with closed eyes. Third, this results in the task of seeing educational equity as an educational policy programme. The discourse of educational science often shies away from this normative perspective, leaving educational policy to (hopefully) make reasonable decisions. The frequently heard position is that it is not the task of science to become normative. In essence, however, this is reductive because in the pedagogical context in particular, it is not only a matter of describing the world as it is but also of setting out how it should be and what would be necessary for it to be. The associated conceptual clarifications are addressed in the following.

What are we actually talking about: education, educational inequalities, educational justice?

The concept of education is not only a terminus technicus within educational science but is also of relevance to educational policy. The constitutions of all the countries of the world contain an article that defines and explains the educational mission of schools. This anchoring is remarkable in so far as it places school and teaching in a legal space which then defines tasks and duties.

In the German state of Bavaria, for example, the educational mandate is formulated in Article 131 of the Bavarian Constitution. There, paragraph 1 states, "Schools shall not only impart knowledge and skills, but also form heart and character". Fundamental to the understanding of education associated with this is the anthropological definition of the human being as a person. In the German Basic Law, this idea is enshrined in Article 1 with the words that human dignity is inviolable. In this respect, not only does every human being have the gift of education, but it is also his or her task. In the context of school and teaching, this results in the duty to support every human being in his or her educational process.

It may sound old-fashioned to name the areas of knowledge and ability on the one hand and heart and character on the other. However, it draws attention to the fact that education must not be limited to individual areas of being human, but that it refers to the entire personality in all its facets. In addition to cognitive aspects, it also involves social, moral, aesthetic, motivational, spiritual, and many other aspects (cf. Gardner, 1983). From this point of view, it is forbidden to limit the human being to only one of these areas, thus possibly using him or her as 'human capital' for external purposes. The human being is a value in itself that is not to be questioned, whose education is not to be instrumentalised. Moreover, the various facets of personality point to the fact that there are interactions and that, against this background, education must always have a comprehensive claim if it wants to do justice to human beings in all their possibilities.

With these considerations, the goal of education is defined: as a gift and task of being human, it has no goal outside itself. Consequently, education is about the human being, about being human and becoming human. This process as such is never complete because the human being is always faced with the challenge of being who he or she is.

This goal is universally valid and therefore not dependent on social changes, although the concretisation of this goal must take social changes into account. This idea becomes particularly clear when one considers how different the starting conditions can be for the individual. This may be illustrated by the following differences: female/male, milieu close to education/milieu far from education, working-class family/academic family, countryside/city, no siblings/many siblings, and so on. The resulting differences with regard to education are called educational inequalities. They thus mark circumstances on the part of the human being that can inhibit or promote the gift and task of being human, depending on the situation. The aforementioned formula of the "Catholic working-class girl from the countryside" is an exaggeration of these educational inequalities, as it encompasses four aspects that were known then as now to be effective: religion, gender, family background, and place of residence.

Educational inequalities are usually only considered from a diagnostic perspective and do not yet provide a goal that can guide educational measures. For this reason, a normative conclusion is needed, which is mostly referred to as educational equity. It is also characterised by complexity. In this respect, a thorough examination of the concept of justice is indispensable. In essence, three perspectives are currently distinguished: first, there is an educational justice that can be characterised as anthropological. It means that every human being has the right to education, regardless of gender, faith, skin colour, origin, and the like. This is an entitlement that is not implemented everywhere in the world and there is still much to do, but at least in most Western countries like UK, Germany, or France, everyone has the right to attend kindergarten and school and, if they meet the performance requirements, to study. Second, there is an educational justice that can be characterised as pedagogical. It means that all people exhibit differences in intelligence, knowledge, ability, motivation, and attitudes. The consequence of this is that learners need different learning opportunities. This is illustrated, for example, by the different branches of the gymnasium and the different directions of vocational education. And third, there is an educational equity that can be characterised as social. It means that under certain circumstances, it is necessary to treat people unequally in order to ensure more justice in society as a whole. A prime example is the promotion of learners from educationally disadvantaged backgrounds: the earlier it is possible to support them, the sooner they can participate in society as a whole. And conversely, targeted support for the best of a cohort can translate into prosperity for society as a whole, which is primarily due to their performance.

Educational inequalities open up opportunities and set limits. From the point of view of educational policy, it is important that the education system does not become an amplifier of these educational inequalities but rather curbs them as far as possible and even has a compensatory effect. Then the education system contributes to educational justice and ensures that all children and young people can be educated according to their possibilities. Incidentally, this has nothing to do with egalitarianism. Quite the contrary: at its core, educational justice is demonstrated by fair inequality based on the principle of equal opportunities. The Covid-19 pandemic, as a once-in-a-lifetime event, has changed so much in society as a whole that the contexts presented have also undergone a re-sorting.

2 The suffering of children and adolescents in the Covid-19 pandemic

If one follows the World Health Organisation (WHO), health is more than the absence of disease. Its constitution from 1946 already states, "Health is a state of complete physical, mental and social well-being". In this respect, the concept of health is characterised by an overarching approach that does not only focus on certain facets of the human being but takes into account all dimensions of the human being and includes the areas of the psyche, the physical, and the social. The psyche includes all of a human being's mental characteristics and personality traits; the physical includes a human being's physical condition, such as strength, endurance, agility, and coordination; and the social includes all aspects of social integration and social participation. Furthermore, it can be seen that these areas influence each other. Although they can be considered in isolation from each other, they are mutually dependent in a person's life. For example, a mental impairment can also have an impact on physical condition and the social component of health.

The parallels to the concept of education as defined in the first chapter are obvious. Education, too, cannot be reduced to individual areas of the personality but refers to the entire personality in all its facets. In addition to cognitive aspects, it also includes social, moral, aesthetic, motivational, spiritual, and many other aspects. Just as the concept of health cannot be limited to just a few areas, the same applies to the concept of education. And just as the various aspects of health are interdependent, the different facets of personality are interdependent. Last but not least, it should be pointed out that both health and education, while not all-encompassing, nevertheless entail to a considerable extent the possibility of being influenced by each individual.

A fulfilled life can be achieved through health and education. If one is lacking, the other has a harder time. If one is lacking too much, the other can no longer be realised. Seen in this light, health and education are intrinsically interdependent, and whenever it becomes apparent in educational policy that one of these areas is falling behind, the need for action is indicated.

DOI: 10.4324/9781003408864-2

If we now take the outlined triad of the concept of health, namely the psyche, the physical, and the social, and then consider the measures that have been taken to contain the Covid-19 pandemic, we see that the health of children and young people has suffered. Children and adolescents had to and still have to suffer. The consequences of this leave visible traces in education.

This chapter, therefore, examines three sub-aspects: First, it discusses the decline in learning performance, which can be seen above all in studies of empirical educational research. Second, it addresses psychological stress, which is indicated by statistics from the health care system. And third, it goes into physical deficits, which can be measured as a result of a reduction in physical activity time combined with an increase in screen time.

The decline in learning performance

At present, one of the most pressing questions from a pedagogical perspective is, What impact do school closures with distance learning have on academic performance? Can teaching under the constraints of the Covid-19 pandemic provide equivalent learning success? This addresses the cognitive perspective. It is about learning growth in the school subjects and thus about knowledge and skills in selected domains. The emphasis on mathematical, scientific-technical, and linguistic competencies is well-known and has been a justified point of criticism ever since PISA (Programme for International Student Assessment) and other such studies. After all, education encompasses more than these three competencies. The reason why this narrowness in research exists from the cognitive perspective is as simple as it is unsatisfactory: because these three competencies can be measured best. And yet, the empirical approach to the cognitive perspective on the basis of selected competency areas is helpful in making well-founded statements about the effectiveness of schools from this perspective. One has to be cautious when extending the results to other subjects and domains or to the education system as a whole.

While many opinions oscillating between apocalypse and euphoria are circulating in the discussion about the influence of school closures with distance teaching on school performance, a look at the research first divides opinions: it must be said that in some countries, such as Germany, hardly any meaningful research has been conducted on the subject for some time. In view of educational policy, this is remarkable. While there is mass testing for Covid-19, there are no comparative performance assessments of students. On the contrary, such assessments are even being cancelled – and thus a great opportunity to finally obtain data for the debate is being lost. The question even arises whether those responsible do not want to know what the school closures have done.

So it is that more and more surveys by institutions close to education are trying to clarify how the back-and-forth between face-to-face teaching under hygienic conditions, hybrid teaching, and distance teaching in schools has affected the learning performance of children and young people. The results are largely unambiguous: everyone is concerned that learners are falling behind. However, as long as empirical data is lacking, it is debatable whether the self-reported and external assessments are really true or not.

Against this background, it is worth taking a look abroad and thus at international research. It may be assumed that due to the similar nature of the measures taken to contain the Covid-19 pandemic all over the world, there is no reason to disregard results from international studies. To this end, a rapid review was carried out in March 2021. It involved presenting a selection of individual studies from different countries and bringing them together by means of statistical procedures (cf. Zierer, 2021c). The aim of such a rapid review is clear: to generate the fastest possible evidence for educational policy decisions while respecting scientific standards.

The dataset includes the learning performance of over four million learners from five countries (Netherlands, Switzerland, Belgium, USA, and Germany) and spans the eight-week period during which schools were closed and switched to distance learning during the first lockdown in 2020. The underlying studies mainly measured mathematical and native language competencies. The studies referred to students in primary and lower secondary education.

The result is clear and not surprising to common sense: in all countries studied, school closures with distance learning have led to a negative effect on students. This decline in academic achievement is evident at both the primary and lower secondary levels, although it affects younger children more than older learners. At the primary level, the learning gaps are comparable to a loss of up to half a school year. At the lower secondary level, the average loss is a quarter of a school year. The decline in academic performance is thus greater than the duration of the lockdown itself because the learning gaps worsened over the course of the school year due to a lack of educational support measures. It is just as noticeable in mathematical competence as in native language competence, and it affects all learners – regardless of age, gender, and performance level. It is noteworthy that the negative effects are even stronger in educationally deprived milieus and can be twice as great depending on educational inequality. Ethnic minorities and low-income families are most affected. The Covid-19 pandemic thus becomes a driver of educational inequality in the education sector.

Several meta-analyses are available as of the beginning of 2023, including data from Australia, Brazil, China, Mexico, Italy, South Africa, and UK too. All of them confirm the results of the rapid review discussed earlier (cf. König et al., 2022; Betthäuser et al., 2023).

Certainly, one should note when interpreting the figures that schools worldwide were not prepared for the lockdown in spring 2020 and that school activities have improved in the meantime. Thus, it can be assumed that the effects in the further weeks of the school lockdown need no longer be so negative. In contrast to this, however, it must be taken into account that the countries studied have all been able to build on a good digitalisation of the education system (cf. Eickelmann et al., 2019) and, moreover, that the school closures covered significantly more than eight weeks for most of the countries. It may be assumed that many learners have been set back by an entire school year.

In the debate about these effects, it is sometimes said that it is not so bad if learners from the primary school sector have negative effects. They still have enough time to make up for lost ground. After all, it is more important that learners in secondary schools have not fallen quite so far behind. However, studies on learning gaps show that avoiding learning gaps in the first place is generally always better for learning success; in other words, prevention should come before intervention. After all, once gaps have occurred, they usually become bigger and bigger because they can only be closed with difficulty and at great financial, organisational, and pedagogical expense. Recent studies of the long-term effects of school closures during the Covid-19 pandemic confirm this (cf. Molnár et al., 2023).

What should not be forgotten is that the available studies have all primarily measured mathematical, scientific, and native language competencies. What has not been researched are all the other subjects and thus all the other cognitive domains: foreign languages, science and technology, politics, economics, social studies, history, and geography, not to mention sports, music, and art. Here, one does not have to be a prophet to draw the conclusion that the learning deficits in these areas are at least as great, but far more likely even greater still. How can learning be successful in subjects that have not been taught? Chance, in the form of an interest or a family background, may have supported one learner or another, but systematic support for all students has not taken place.

All in all, it remains to be said: From an educational point of view, the Covid-19 pandemic and its measures have led to a decline in learning performance, which affects all learners, but especially children and young people from educationally deprived backgrounds. Moreover, all subjects are affected, even those that received special attention during the pandemic, such as mathematics and native language education. In order to be able to avert an educational catastrophe from the point of view of subject learning, concrete measures of individual support are indispensable.

Mental stress

The focus on learning performance may be justified, but education encompasses more than this, and human health, as already mentioned, spans a broader spectrum than just the cognitive. Especially important for young people is their psychosocial development.

Despite all the justified criticism, the stage model of human psychosocial development by Joan Erikson and Erik H. Erikson (1966) is still relevant today. It distinguishes between eight stages, each of which describes a field of tension between the needs and desires of the human being as an individual on the one hand and the constantly changing demands of the social environment on the other hand. Since this field of tension of each stage has to be resolved, and the person, therefore, progresses to the next stage either strengthened or weakened, Joan Erikson and Erik H. Erikson also speak of crises that have to be mastered without finally being overcoming. Every crisis persists in a person's life, albeit in the background. It is problematic for a person's psychosocial development if he or she emerges weakened from a crisis because this hinders further phases of life. This weakening also occurs when a crisis has not been experienced at all.

What are the eight crises (cf. Zierer, 2021b)? In the first stage (first year of life), the poles are primal trust versus primal mistrust. The child is born relatively unprotected and therefore needs closeness, affection, security, and safety. If the child does not experience all this, it develops fear and mistrust. In the second stage (second and third year of life), the crisis is determined by autonomy on the one hand and shame and doubt on the other hand. The child expands its range of action and becomes more active on its own. The more trust it has in its environment, the more autonomous it will become. If there are many setbacks in this stage or if the necessary basic trust is lacking, the child's self-concept is damaged insofar as it becomes negatively occupied and flooded with insecurity. In the third stage (fourth and fifth year of life), the conscience is formed in a special way in the area of tension between initiative versus a feeling of guilt. This can be steered towards fear and feeling guilty by strictness and prohibitions, which is a hindrance to further development. It is more beneficial if the child is allowed to be proactive in a familiar space and mistakes are not seen as a flaw but as an opportunity to learn. The fourth stage (sixth year to puberty) is about the relationship between a sense of achievement and a sense of inferiority. People at this age no longer just want to watch and observe; they also want to make, produce, create something. Joan Erikson and Erik H. Erikson call this the sense of work. People who only experience failure in this phase or who are not given the opportunity to develop their sense of work develop a feeling of inferiority. In this respect, the tasks should not be too difficult, but also not too easy. This is the challenge that drives and, if successful, leads to an increase in self-concept. In the fifth stage (adolescence), the person is faced with the task of finding his or her role in the community with peers. In view of numerous pitfalls, this is no easy task. It becomes particularly clear that those who have not mastered the preceding stages are especially challenged in this stage. If a person fails here too, the result is an ego identity diffusion instead of an ego identity. In the sixth stage (early adulthood), the task is to achieve a certain level of intimacy and not to fall into social isolation. This is a prerequisite for love, which takes on central importance in adulthood. If a person does not manage to open up to others, make friends, and be faithful, loneliness can be the result. In the seventh stage (adulthood), Joan Erikson and Erik H. Erikson speak of generativity versus stagnation and self-absorption. By this they mean the positive outcome of the crisis, that people are ready to bring children into the world and show social commitment. Those who fail in this stage will withdraw and deal primarily with themselves. The eighth and last stage (mature adulthood) brings with it the challenge for people to look back on their lives and prepare for death. If the view is characterised by contentment, the end of life is also accepted. Dissatisfaction, on the other hand, leads to despair and the feeling of having to live longer or once more.

Again, one does not have to be a prophet to venture the prediction that the measures to contain the Covid-19 pandemic are a hindrance to being able to cope with the developmental tasks described by Joan Erikson and Erik H. Erikson: Those who become socially isolated, no longer have any contacts, can no longer meet friends, and have to constantly keep their distance are faced with difficult conditions. Cultural anthropological studies have shown, for example, that there is something like a cultural distance between people that signals how close at least and how far at most they need to be to be able to work, play, and learn with each other. For no culture in this world is this 1.50 metres when it comes to friendship. Virologically, therefore, the distance may make sense, but pedagogically it does not.

The effects of the measures to contain the Covid-19 pandemic on the psyche of children and young people can be illustrated with the help of various research data. The first are the data on an extreme situation, but one that has become reality for many thousands of schoolchildren: quarantine. The fact that it makes epidemiological sense does not need to be discussed here. Rather, from a pedagogical point of view, the question arises, Can quarantine also have negative consequences?

In retrospect, one has to rub one's eyes in disbelief that teachers' associations did not ask this question. Instead, they became chief virologists in the crisis and almost unanimously called for schools to be closed. Where has the pedagogical ethos gone? Where is the Socratic Oath? One may argue about Hartmut von Hentig (2003), but his reformulation of the Hippocratic Oath is groundbreaking for teachers:

As a teacher, I pledge to respect the peculiarities of every child and to defend them against everyone; to stand up for their physical and mental integrity; to pay attention to their impulses, to listen to them, to take them seriously; to seek their consent to everything I do to their person, as I would to an adult.

How does quarantine work and what does it do to young people? They are not asked. The health department decides by notice and maybe contacts them by phone – that's it for social contacts. It is not dialogue that rules, but dictation. This may be justifiable in view of certain threatening scenarios, but a look at how young people experience quarantine should not be missing. There has long been research on this. As early as May 2020, a group of researchers led by Susanne Röhr published a study with clear results: depression, anxiety, anger, stress, post-traumatic stress, loneliness, and stigmatisation are common psychosocial problems. Even suicide cannot be ruled out. So the possible protection of society harms the individual. Is this solidarity? At least it reminds us of its perverse power, as Richard Sennett calls it.

Without a doubt, some make it through quarantine without any problems. In "Ein Lied für Jetzt" [A Song for Now], the German band Die Ärzte describe their experience: "That little bit of quarantine is not the worst thing in the world". For some children and young people, however, it is exactly that. Because they need social contact in their personality development more than adults. The worries they have are just as threatening to their existence as the possible reproaches they may receive – there are politicians who rhetorically ask children in all seriousness whether they want to be blamed for the death of their grandmother. Young people have to find their role, for which peers are crucial – not so much siblings or parents, even if they can provide balance. But a proper quarantine also excludes these people. For example, the following applied in the autumn of 2020 in the German state of Bavaria: "The child should, as far as possible for its age, keep away from other family members in the home, if possible in a separate room with its own bathroom and toilet. Close physical contact should be avoided as far as possible". Children and adolescents need closeness and security, especially in times of crisis, social isolation, and worry. Those who advocate locking them away and not giving them the opportunity to be physically active outdoors are perverting their mental, physical, and social health.

As important as quarantine can be, it must always be done in consideration of the individual case in order to be proportionate. Sending children and young people into quarantine across the board does not achieve the goal of responsible action. The most important step towards this goal is education: people who know why they are doing something act responsibly. Senseless and incomprehensible restrictions provoke the opposite.

From a pedagogical point of view, thoughtful guidance is essential right from the start. Leaving families alone can ignite an inferno in social hotspots.

Quarantine is certainly an extreme situation for keeping one's distance, but one that nevertheless vividly demonstrates the psychological consequences. But even the less drastic measures for containing the Covid-19 pandemic can have a negative impact on the development and education of children and young people. Thus, numerous surveys (cf. Ravens-Sieberer et al., 2021; Fegert et al., 2020; Andresen et al., 2020; Bignardi et al., 2020; Damerow et al., 2020; Schlack et al., 2020; Panda et al., 2021) of children, adolescents, and adults indicate that, for example, anxiety, depression, loneliness, irritability, insomnia, headaches, low mood, abdominal pain, and nervousness have increased significantly in all age groups during the Covid-19 pandemic compared to surveys from earlier years. These results are found worldwide and again affect children and young people from educationally deprived milieus more severely. If more than half of the children and young people today report some of the problems mentioned and thus the percentages have doubled compared to previous years, then the tendency is clear: the crisis is putting a strain on people's psyche, and the longer it lasts, the more negative the consequences.

Of course, the significance of surveys and self-reports is lower compared to medical findings. Therefore, figures from health insurance companies (e.g., DAK, 2021; Barmer, 2021; DPtV, 2021), for example, are all the more important: in 2020, there were more days of absence due to mental illness than ever before, and more and more children and young people are undergoing psychological and psychotherapeutic treatment.

Whether all this has led to an increase in domestic violence, especially towards children, is still a matter of debate. Admittedly, there are many reports and initial studies (cf. Steinert et al., 2020; Fegert et al., 2020) that suggest this conclusion. However, the statistics are not consistent. In Germany, for example, a press release by the Senate Department for Justice, Consumer Protection, and Anti-Discrimination from 3 March 2021 states that fewer cases are reported in the Berlin violence protection outpatient clinic during a lockdown but that their number rises again sharply after a lockdown. One explanation for this is that it is more difficult for victims to leave their own homes to seek help during a lockdown. Despite these ripples in the statistics, a general increase in domestic violence can be observed – not only since the Covid-19 pandemic but continuously in recent years (cf. BKA, 2019).

And one last point is worth noting in the context of mental health: at the beginning of January, paediatricians and school psychologists spoke out. Not only did they warn of already clearly observable learning deficits and gaps in knowledge, but they above all pointed to a growing number of truants. Truancy is one of the most challenging problems in the education system because there are often several causes that have developed over a longer period of time (cf. Ricking et al., 2016). So it is certainly not easy to correct.

In the Covid-19 pandemic, as Nina Großmann from Baden-Württemberg's State Association of School Psychologists (Landesverband der Schulpsychologinnen und Schulpsychologen Baden-Württemberg) puts it in a German press report dated 1 January 2021, students of all ages had become accustomed to doing nothing at home, had neglected their tasks, and felt overwhelmed when they returned to the classroom. A quarter of the cases in the 28 counselling centres in the German state of Baden-Württemberg were due to this phenomenon. Before the crisis, this proportion was about 5 per cent.

Indications of this change in learning behaviour, which is reflected in a lower motivation to learn and a decrease in learning time at school, can also be found in other surveys (cf. Wößmann et al., 2020; mpfs, 2020; Unger et al., 2020).

In view of this data, there is no doubt that the measures to contain the Covid-19 pandemic are leading to psychological stress in children and young people. The crisis also makes young people mentally ill in the long run. It damages their psychosocial development and thus education. In order to avert an impending educational catastrophe in this area, more phases of pedagogically initiated social learning are necessary in the future: children and young people urgently need time and space to play and work together, to learn and celebrate.

The physical deficits

It is probably one of the most quoted sayings from antiquity: "Mens sana in corpore sano". It goes back to the Roman poet Juvenal, who wrote in one of his satires: "Orandum est, ut sit mens sana in corpore sano" [Pray that there may be a sound mind in a sound body]. It was only later that this saying became a common expression for drawing attention to the fact that man does not only have a body to carry his head around. Rather, the human being is an entity with a body, a soul, and a spirit, and in this respect, the physical is just as important as the cognitive.

This connection plays a role in the understanding of health, as well as in the concept of education. The educational mission of schools has always included not only the cognitive areas but also the physical development of the human being. This becomes particularly clear at the German gymnasium, which is the type of school offering the highest level of education in the country. According to the origin of the word, gymnasium means a place of physical and mental training; in ancient times, the main focus was on the physical.

What influence do the measures to contain the Covid-19 pandemic have on the physical development of children and young people? This question, too, does not seem to be of central importance in view of the dominance of learning performance in certain subjects since PISA and others. Meanwhile, especially in times of crisis, the question of bodily integrity has become the focus of public debates – unfortunately, it is discussed only one-sidedly from a virological point of view, but not against the background of pedagogical considerations.

If we take a look at the lives of students during the Covid-19 pandemic, we can see the harbingers of an educational catastrophe in this area: distance learning meant that there was no longer any need to go to school, which for many children and adolescents was an important counterbalance to the sedentary activity at school itself, both in the morning and at lunchtime or in the afternoon. Next, many students were tied up in front of monitors all morning in their children's rooms and the small flats. During these times, the learners often did not use breaks to simply go outside because there were no friends around to motivate them to do so. Instead, they continued to sit in their rooms and endure hours of video conferencing. Looking out of the window was often the only change from staring at the screen. Ironic references were also made to 'lying down to study' and to having a 'bedtop' instead of a laptop, pointing out that many learners did not even make it to their desks.

As always with such descriptions, there is a risk of exaggeration. But there is already a body of research that backs up the exaggerations with evidence. First, studies (cf. Damerow et al., 2020; Schmidt et al., 2020; Wößmann et al., 2020; Nowossadeck et al., 2021) unanimously report that organised physical activity, especially that which takes place in sports clubs, has fallen victim to the lockdown measures and thus often declined to zero. However, there was an increase in all age groups in everyday exercise activities, such as walking, cycling, gardening, and the like. So on balance, children and adolescents actually spent more time moving outside in the fresh air during the Covid-19 pandemic.

Against this background, one might well conclude that physical fitness did not suffer during the crisis. However, this impression is deceptive when further data are added. For example, the studies mentioned indicate that there are effects of the educational milieu, just as there are effects of the decline in learning performance and the increase in psychological stress. Specifically, people who were already active in sports before the Covid-19 pandemic used the time available at home to be even more active in sports. Passive people, on the other hand, benefited less from the new time slots. So here, too, educational inequality is increasing.

Furthermore, it can be observed that despite an increase in everyday exercise, body weight increased across all age groups and all educational milieus (cf. Damerow et al., 2020; Nowossadeck et al., 2021). More everyday exercise, therefore, does not necessarily lead to better physical development. This is not least due to the fact that everyday exercise does not correspond to systematic training, especially in younger people, and is thus less effective than organised exercise despite a longer duration (cf. López-Bueno et al., 2021).

Two further reasons need to be addressed at this point because they once again reinforce educational inequalities and thus lead to more educational injustice.

First, the measures implemented to contain Covid-19 have had an impact on the diet of children and young people (cf. Koletzko et al., 2021). Since the beginning of the crisis, young people have been eating more sweets, but also more fruit. Boys are more prone to unhealthy eating habits than girls, and as a result, they also gain more weight. The less educated the home, the more unhealthy the diet and the greater the weight gain among children.

Second, the measures taken to curb Covid have led to an increase in screen time among children and adolescents across all age groups and all educational milieus (cf. Schmidt et al., 2020; Wößmann et al., 2020). Since the daily time for school-based learning has simultaneously decreased, these additional times have been used for extracurricular activities, such as television, computer games, and social media. Again, a greater negative effect is seen for children and young people with lower learning achievements from disadvantaged families: they watch more TV, surf the internet pointlessly, learn less, do not exercise enough, and eat poorly. All in all, then, the Covid-19 pandemic has become a driver of educational injustice from this perspective as well.

To conclude the remarks on physical deficits, I would like to present a study that sums up the whole dilemma of school closures in terms of physical development (cf. Wang et al., 2021): in China, the visual acuity of six- to eight-year-old students is measured every year. In 2020, distance learning was in place between January and May, and learners worked on computers at home. The result was a measurable increase in myopia among the youngest by almost four times compared to previous years.

It is true that an increase in myopia has been observed for years in many countries. Reading is also a close-distance activity, but the increased use of tablets and others as a result of school closures means that close-distance activities are increasing, and more and more children are becoming short-sighted. Looking out of the window into the distance has become a rarity; the eyes are more likely to turn to the smartphone and thus once again remain at close range. The increase in short-sightedness, especially among young people, is a serious health risk in the long run. This is because the earlier myopia occurs, the more likely it is to cause consequential damage such as retinal detachment and glaucoma. Encouraging in this context is the result of a study from Taiwan (cf. Wu et al.,

2018): spending 120 minutes a day outdoors has both a preventive and an intervening effect. Pedagogically, therefore, this physical impairment can be tackled.

While the severity of Covid-19 disease in children is still a matter of debate, it is already certain today that the measures taken to contain Covid-19 have been detrimental to the physical development of children and adolescents. In order to avert an impending educational catastrophe in this area, increased phases of pedagogically initiated physical learning will be necessary in the future: more than ever, children and young people need time and space for play, sport, and movement.

3 Approaches to averting the impending educational catastrophe

Without wanting to be alarmist, the signs of the times indicate that an educational catastrophe is looming: The learning performance of children and young people cannot be promoted in distance teaching in the same way as in face-to-face teaching. In addition, learning behaviour has been damaged, which is more serious in that this forms the basis for learning performance and can hardly be compensated for. Social behaviour has also been thrown off track by the lack of school rules and rituals, as well as social contacts. Finally, there are physical deficits as a result of reduced mobility and increased screen activity.

If not now, when? This is the question one is inclined to ask from an educational perspective in view of the data. Countermeasures must be taken immediately to support all children and young people – especially those from educationally deprived milieus because the deficits are far greater there. It is therefore all the more gratifying that there is no longer only a debate about the digital upgrading of children's rooms in the Covid-19 pandemic but also about educational measures. An example is the German federal government's tutoring programme, which was announced in March 2021 and is to be financed with one billion euros. The need for these discussions was not seen by everyone from the beginning, although there were early indications. Floating on the digitalisation cloud, many believed that the crisis would finally give the school system the digital boost it needed to solve all its problems at once.

As is always the case in educational policy discourse, people are quick to look at structural approaches to solving the problem, thereby committing the error in thinking that empirical education research has been pointing out for decades: Structural measures alone will not bring about learning success because what is decisive is what happens in the structures or, to put it another way, how good the teaching is.

What has been said applies decisively to a much-discussed approach: retention. It is quickly seen as a cure-all for combating learning deficits. This is because learners could claim a retention without it being credited as a repetition year and simply repeat the lost school year. However, if one

DOI: 10.4324/9781003408864-3

takes a look at the current ranking of John Hattie's 'Visible Learning' (cf. Zierer, 2021a), a data set with over 95,000 individual studies and thus one of the largest syntheses of empirical educational research, it becomes clear that retention is one of the measures that have the least effect and that it even has a considerable negative effect on student learning performance and also on learning and social behaviour. Why is this so? As a rule, the process of retention is such that learners are taken out of their familiar class group and placed in a new one, where they have to learn again what they have already learned. But what these learners need is not more of the same curriculum, the same tasks, and the same experiences. What they need is something different: teaching that enables them to learn, that motivates them, challenges them, and always spurs them on to make an effort and get involved. It is not only about challenging and supporting them professionally but about changing their attitude towards learning. Failure to move up often only invites them to do the work again – with the same unsatisfactory results.

So giving students in crisis the option of repeating a grade may seem obvious at first glance. At second glance, however, research shows that this approach is not very promising: Why should a measure be effective now, of all times, when it has been known for years that it does not work? Those who nevertheless want to stick to this option will have to give a lot of thought to the pedagogical design. For example, how are learners tested in advance? A meaningful diagnosis is the basis of any support. Here, the nationwide comparative tests could help to determine what has really been learned and where the gaps are. A number of questions would have to be answered: what methods of support are available? Well-thought-out learning paths would be the least that could be effective. They are not yet available, so they would have to be developed. What kind of grouping is aimed at? Simply sending the learners to a new class is not enough. Small groups, formed according to the tasks, would be essential. How are teachers prepared for this? Grade retention is an unknown quantity in teacher training, so professionalisation in this area would be necessary. And finally, how are parents involved in the process? They are crucial for success in school, especially in the case of failure, so it would also be necessary to consider cooperation with parents.

So many questions remain. They demand an answer. Otherwise, a well-intentioned measure may not only remain ineffective in the end but even do harm. In terms of educational policy, it is therefore appropriate to pick up the pace considerably on the issue of addressing learning deficits.

The discussed example of a possible measure to reduce learning deficits makes it clear that the complexity of educational processes cannot be met with simple formulas. Rather, measures are needed at different levels in order to be successful in the short, medium, and long term.

This chapter will therefore, first, discuss which new structures are necessary for support concepts to be effective, second, explain to what extent people need to be strengthened in order for the new structures to work, and, third, outline what professionalisation of teaching must look like against this background. These points intend to avoid a mistake that was characteristic of the failure of so many well-intentioned measures in the wake of the educational catastrophe of the 1960s – namely, the almost exclusive focus on structures and the associated overlooking of the necessary quality within these structures. The three steps "create structures – strengthen people – professionalise teaching" must be the guiding principle of educational policy. Structures alone are not enough if those involved in them are not empowered to use them.

Creating structures

In view of the deficits in the mental, physical, and social development of children and young people, one of the most important tasks for the coming weeks and months, perhaps even years, will be to set up structures for individual support and to create comprehensive educational spaces for cognitive, social, and physical learning.

Promising structural measures for individual support are available from the past – for example, summer schools, afternoon courses, or homework supervision. Against the backdrop of an impending educational catastrophe, the all-day school is also being reassessed, as it combines a number of the approaches mentioned and brings them together to form a coherent whole.

At first glance, the aforementioned concepts, such as summer school, afternoon classes, homework supervision, and also all-day school, achieve only moderate effects on average (cf. Hattie et al., 2019). In view of their costs, this is a sobering picture. At second glance, however, it becomes apparent that on the one hand, the effects mentioned can be ascertained for all students – regardless of educational milieu, type of school, age, subject, and the like – and on the other hand, greater differences in the effects are a consequence of the quality of the measures. So there are summer schools, afternoon courses, and homework supervision that are done well – and unfortunately also ones that are done poorly.

What are the distinguishing features of successful measures? In other words, what is decisive for the success of a summer school, an afternoon course, or homework supervision? The findings of empirical educational research are important, especially against the background of the urgent structural reforms for reducing educational deficits and for more educational justice.

Making summer schools attractive and effective

Since the research findings point in one direction across all the measures mentioned, it is sufficient to use the example of summer schools to illustrate the core messages: summer schools were conceived in the USA in particular. Despite demonstrable successes, this tradition has been adopted only sporadically in other countries. The original aim of summer schools was to mitigate the negative effects that can be observed every year as a result of summer holidays. Today, there are other reasons for introducing summer school. What they have in common is the elimination of learning deficits. They differ in terms of the target group of the learners, so at least four types of summer schools can be mentioned.

First, there are summer schools that help students to compensate for deficits from the current school year and to stabilise the minimum requirements for promotion. Second, there are summer schools in which learners repeat a subject they did not pass during the school year. Third, summer schools are offered for learners with special needs in order to provide them with support beyond the normal level of instruction. And fourth, summer schools aim to reach learners from socially disadvantaged families in order to alleviate existing educational inequalities and ensure greater educational equity.

In the USA, the offerings have expanded as summer schools have become more established. They are no longer designed only to address learning deficits. Summer schools are now also offered to learners who are unable to attend classes regularly due to extracurricular commitments – for example, because they are active in competitive sports. Likewise, summer schools are open to learners who want to progress faster in the education system. In the 1960s, for example, when there was a shortage of space in schools due to the baby boom, summer schools were seen as a way to speed up graduation to make room for the growing number of students. In recent years, summer holidays have been seen as an ideal time to offer special programmes for high-ability learners. Consequently, these summer schools are not about remediating learning deficits but about acceleration – that is, advanced instruction. Unlike summer schools that address learning deficits, summer schools for acceleration are usually not free of charge but have a fee or are part of a scholarship programme. Due to the insecure employment situation of teachers in the USA, summer schools offer an additional source of income.

The effectiveness of summer schools has now been extensively researched. The synthesis in Visible Learning (cf. Hattie et al., 2019; Zierer, 2019), the largest data set in empirical educational research, is based on three meta-analyses comprising a total of 105 individual studies. From these data, it can be concluded that summer schools have a positive impact on student learning performance in both cases presented: in addressing learning deficits and in accelerating. Given the effort behind implementing a summer school, the effect may seem small at first glance. However, a second look at the details of the research reveals – as is so often the case with structural measures – that it is above all the interaction between all those involved that determines the success of a measure. For this reason, it is worth taking a closer look at the implementation. Finally, this can be used to derive general consequences for individual support.

Although students from all social milieus can make learning progress in a summer school, the effects are greater for learners from middle and higher educational levels than for those from educationally disadvantaged milieus. The reason for this is the so-called Matthew effect, according to which learners can benefit more from educational opportunities due to certain family and social support mechanisms. These support mechanisms are often lacking for children and young people from educationally disadvantaged backgrounds. Nevertheless, it should be noted that learners from educationally disadvantaged backgrounds benefit from summer schools even under existing circumstances and that it is right to make a targeted offering for this group, especially in the interest of improving educational equity.

Summer schools are all the more effective when the learning group is smaller. If the courses are too large, the learning gains dwindle. If further research is taken into consideration, an effective group size is probably a maximum of five learners. The crucial question in this context is how teachers succeed in setting challenging goals in the smaller learning groups, motivating students, engaging them in exchange, and obtaining and giving effective feedback.

With regard to learning performance, it can be seen that positive effects are achieved by summer schools in all subjects studied. Although these are generally somewhat higher in mathematics than in language teaching, in view of the importance of language for learning success at school and participation in society, one should not conclude from this that the associated use of summer schools would not be worthwhile. Instead, two characteristics of effective summer schools should be mentioned here: on the one hand, a targeted diagnosis is helpful if one is to provide learners with programmes that really help them. These programmes must not be too difficult or too easy, but they should be challenging. On the other hand, supporting subject-specific learning with meta-cognitive strategies is particularly conducive to learning – for example, it must be clarified how the learners deal with mistakes, what they do when stuck, how they proceed in problem-solving, and what problem-solving procedures they use. Both aspects can be observed not only in summer schools but in school learning in general.

Finally, the research findings indicate that regionally implemented summer schools are more effective than nationally implemented ones. The reason for this is that smaller programmes give those responsible more flexibility to tailor teaching, especially the content of lessons, to the specific needs of the learners and their specific context. Centralised control often prevents these opportunities. As is so often the case with structural issues, the cost-benefit ratio must be seen in a field of tension in which too large can become just as detrimental as too small.

Reasons cited by parents and teachers for the failure of summer programmes include the short-term nature of decision-making and the resulting pressure to plan, as well as the failure of needed materials to arrive on time. These problems are more common in large programmes and are solvable through increased financial support.

Regarding the role of parents, the research findings suggest that their involvement in the summer school is important. This is especially the case because learning success is always dependent on the family background. In particular, learners who attend summer school to address learning deficits usually experience little support from their parents. Making these parents aware of how important they are for their children's learning must therefore be part of successful summer school programmes and can be facilitated through parent courses and parents' evenings.

Another factor that impairs the effectiveness of summer schools is a lack of progress surveys and insufficient monitoring of activities. Thus, it is important to conduct regular interim surveys to continually adjust the level of teaching to the learners' abilities and to monitor the completion of tasks and attendance.

The research findings provide clear guidelines for policymakers, especially on the funding, development, and implementation of summer schools. There is no doubt that summer schools lead to positive effects. Only at first glance do they appear to be not particularly high. At second glance, these effects are not negligible – especially as they usually benefit learners who would otherwise fall further behind academically. Moreover, it is likely that summer schools have positive effects that go far beyond those observed in previous research. For children living in areas of high crime and poverty, summer schools provide a safe and stimulating environment that is clearly preferable to the alternatives. Summer schools can thus curb youth delinquency. For single-parent families and families in which both parents work outside the home, summer schools perform a caregiving function.

There are various approaches to increasing the attractiveness of summer schools. It is promising to establish summer schools not as an additional offering but as a fixed component of the school profile. This initiates a cultural change which is important for schools in general: individual support is not something special, an exception, or an emergency programme. Rather, it is perfectly natural in school learning to challenge oneself again and again and to continue working. In order to ensure quality, regular evaluation is necessary, which can then be directed outwards with positive results to underline the attractiveness for learners and their families.

The so-called cultural framing (in the form of festivals and celebrations, joint activities, etc.) has been little examined so far in research on the effectiveness of summer schools. However, the general state of research on this complex of topics shows that cultural framing is an important element in making school not only a place of learning but also an educational space. The joy of learning is just as important as the effectiveness of learning. First and foremost, outdoor and adventure education measures should be mentioned in this context, such as reading nights, tent camps, and class trips. They can, indeed must, be integrated into programmes for individual support. The effects are positive in all areas studied: on mathematical, scientific, and linguistic competencies, on social competencies, on self-concept, and on motivation to learn. And there is another special feature of outdoor and adventure education measures: They have follow-up effects and retain their influence beyond the measure. This is rare in educational science. Usually, a so-called wash-out effect occurs, according to which the influence of a measure can no longer be proven after a certain period of time – for example, in many early childhood development programmes. The demand in the face of an impending educational catastrophe is obvious: in future, every class must receive an outdoor or adventure education measure at least once a school year. This promotes not only subject-specific learning but also social and physical development. And in teacher training, this topic must be treated from the very beginning – teachers who cannot imagine being out of school for a week with their class must be asked to reconsider their choice of profession.

There are many possible ways to find staff for summer schools. For example, summer schools can be implemented with the school's teaching staff as well as with staff from outside the school. In both cases, it is important to prepare staff for summer school because the context of learning is different than in regular school settings due to group size, learning times, and objectives. The coupling of summer schools and teacher training is successfully implemented in many places. For example, teachers might learn new methods in the afternoon, which they can then try out the next morning. The idea of a 'flying start' is interesting in this context: by moving part of the summer school to the beginning of the school year, schools can shorten the time for repetition for the new school year and resume work more quickly. In addition, teachers who will be teaching the participants of the summer school in the new school year could get to know them in advance and thus work on relationships. A 'flying start' of this kind can benefit not only the summer school learners but all learners in a class.

The described facets of a successful summer school can be seen as a master plan for individual support. They also apply to afternoon classes and homework supervision, and even have their place in successful all-day school concepts. In essence, this is about the aforementioned cultural change, according to which individual support is no longer something special or an exception or an emergency programme but something that should be taken for granted at school. Such measures are certainly necessary to prevent the looming educational catastrophe. But they also open up the opportunity to rethink school at precisely this point and to develop it sustainably for the benefit of the learners.

Bringing school television into the digital age

One supporting measure for summer schools, afternoon courses, and homework supervision could be school television. It was introduced as early as the 1960s when television was gaining in importance. Supporting it in Germany, for example, was Georg Picht's discussions of the educational catastrophe that was feared at the time. The regional public broadcaster Bayerischer Rundfunk launched its service in 1964, followed by the regional broadcaster Westdeutscher Rundfunk in 1969. By 1972, the programme was shown nationwide. The development was similar in Austria and Switzerland. ORF, Austria's nationwide television station, and SRF, Switzerland's nationwide television station, regularly broadcast a programme for schools from 1964 on.

A special offering in this context was the so-called Telekolleg. This was conceived as a measure for adult education and pursued the goal of enabling people from rural areas, especially women, to obtain the secondary school leaving certificate or the entrance qualification for a university of applied sciences. A clear commitment to more educational equity was thus the impetus for the Telekolleg. It was initiated by the German state of Bavaria. Several states quickly joined in. Today, however, the Telekolleg is only offered in the German states of Bavaria and Brandenburg. In Bavaria alone, more than 65,000 people were able to obtain one of the degrees mentioned.

Currently, Telekolleg is legally and institutionally anchored in many places. In the wake of school closures as part of the measures to contain Covid, several countries in Europe have relaunched school television: In Austria, for example, '*Freistunde*' (free period) was broadcast for three hours every morning for students aged 10 and above, supplemented with online materials. There were also corresponding platforms in Portugal and Switzerland. The BBC in England took a particularly comprehensive approach with 'BBC Bitesize', creating a complete media library along the curriculum content for all grades and all subjects and also making it possible to structure the day around fixed broadcasting times. The German public broadcasters also compiled a programme on the internet, but this was largely offered in isolation from distance learning.

With regard to the research on school television, the first thing to note is that there are hardly any studies (e.g., Boum, 2003). The few that do exist show the possibilities of school television, as well as its limitations. School television can lead to an increase in learning across the board if it has certain characteristics. In any case, the prerequisite is a functioning structure – that is, secure reception, terminal equipment for all learners, and reliable structures for sending learning materials. One of the central aspects is the quality of the broadcasts: how do they address the students? Do they succeed in motivating students? How is the didactic reduction of the content? Which possibilities of audio-visual processing are used? Successful school television is accompanied by direct support services. Learners have the opportunity to communicate with a teacher during designated times and also to exchange information with each other. In addition, comprehensive learning materials are important, including effective diagnostic procedures as well as exercises and feedback opportunities. So here, too, the question of quality is crucial and not the provision of the structure per se. The most effective programmes are those that always include classroom phases in addition to school TV. This makes it possible to harness the power of peers and also integrate the role of teachers in all its facets.

Compared to the past, the technical framework conditions are much better today: every household has access to television, and while fast internet access is not yet available everywhere, it is becoming more and more common. Despite all the pedagogical reservations about television, it could have been a saviour during the crisis and could help after the Covid-19 pandemic to ensure more educational equity across the board – not just as a 'boob tube', not just as a 'TV on' approach, but thanks to digitalisation in a comprehensive and multifaceted way. Digitalisation could revolutionise school television. What would it have to look like?

Many broadcasters are already offering programmes, but the key step is missing: for each grade level, a crisis timetable could be developed by the ministries, with fixed, focused, and regular broadcasting times. These could be didactically prepared in such a way that students receive at least the most important input across the board and could be expanded by digital offerings, such as quizzes and portfolios. Cooperation phases among learners could also be integrated via numerous platforms. Teachers could thus concentrate on the essentials of distance learning: obtaining and giving feedback. Whether the assignments are then sent by post, handed in at the school during a completion drive, or submitted digitally, none of that would matter. Through a clever rhythmisation in 20-minute sequences and a didactic preparation at the highest level (with learning level surveys and tests), the minimum standards could be taught in all subjects and all grades. This would give learners a structure, teachers support, and parents relief. Of course, this cannot be done overnight. But there are so many committed teachers. Why not unite them to set up such an emergency programme in the short time available? Not every teacher has to reinvent the wheel in a laborious individual effort.

Educational policy could take the lead and finally prove its strength. In the longer term, school TV could be expanded and supplemented with digital tools so that it can also be helpful after the crisis – for differentiation and support, for preparation and follow-up of lessons, for targeted support in the context of a summer school, for an afternoon course or homework supervision. It would even be a useful supplementary measure for a repeat year or for skipping a class. It is precisely the digital tools that are important in all the measures mentioned and that can thus also take on a hinge function.

There is no question that even school television cannot replace classroom instruction: social contact is the decisive educational elixir, and it is missing. School television is therefore intended on the one hand for emergency use and on the other hand to deepen and supplement normal use. Together with the other structural measures, it could help to cushion, or perhaps even prevent, an educational catastrophe.

Long overdue: the convening of an education council

For educational policy to provide the necessary leadership, there needs to be an education council that brings scientific knowledge and practical school experience to the ministries and supports decision-making with theoretical and practical reason and all-round empiricism.

Looking back at the years between 2020 and 2022, it is more than surprising why regular consultations on the Covid-19 pandemic have been held with virologists and epidemiologists but not with representatives of the educational, social, and cultural sciences, as well as people from educational and teaching practice.

The basic idea of an advisory body of this kind is not new, as can be shown with the example of Germany. The German Education Council for example, which was established in 1965 but abolished in 1975, pursued a similar goal. It was composed of people who were active in the fields of church, industry, trade unions, and science. They could independently seek out topics that were considered urgent and of political relevance. The German Education Council was initially a success story, as it was able to exert a decisive influence on public debates and also professional discussions through important publications. Only later did criticism mount, especially from the administration and politics. The German Education Council ultimately fell victim to this back-and-forth.

Looking back on this development, there is much to be learned for the current debate on reconvening an education council. First of all, it should be noted that it was not the basic idea that failed. Despite all priorities of party politics, fundamental questions of educational policy must not fall victim to political power relations. They must be based on the values of the German Basic Law and apply equally to all people of a country. The question of educational justice is such a fundamental question of educational policy.

Next, it can be seen that the political situation has developed in favour of an education council. Whereas in the 1970s the rifts between the parties were almost insurmountable, especially in the field of education, today more common ground can be observed. In addition, a number of transnational issues have already been initiated and are supported by all parties – inclusion, digitalisation, and sustainability are examples of this.

What still needs to be worked on, then as now, is the well-known problem of the difference between theory and practice: who benefits from the best theory if it cannot be implemented in practice? And what good is the best practice if it has no empirical effect? It is precisely in the composition of an education council that the various protagonists in the education system must therefore be included: learners, parents, teachers, educational scientists in the broadest sense, trade unions, administrators, and political parties. Historically, to take up the above example again, the German Education Council also failed due to the resistance of the latter. Even within the individual groups, a careful selection will have to be made, as these are not homogeneous groups. An example of this is the many currents in educational science alone, which combine humanistic approaches and empirical research.

And, finally, prudence is required in the assignment of tasks: should it be an advisory body without binding force or even a body with the possibility of bringing about political decisions? Whatever one decides, it will be important to not define the education council as a body with direct political decision-making power because otherwise it would lose its independence from political power relations and thus also its advisory function. What has been said implies that the education council can and must do both: seek out topics for itself, but also be open to topics according to mandate.

Clearly, an education council in countries with a federal structure, as is the case in the USA and Germany, faces special but not insurmountable challenges. Understood in this way, an education council can optimise the processes of the state ministers of education – and it was precisely the confusion at this level during the Covid-19 pandemic that demonstrated how important a joint advisory body on education issues would be. The bottom line is that just having a common forum for debate on education is so valuable that the convening of an education council should not be dropped.

Change and lighten the load on curricula

The aforementioned measures for individual support cannot be decoupled from the discussion about the abundance of material in the curricula. Thus, an obvious reaction in times of school closures was to teach only the core subjects to the greatest possible extent and to focus only on learning content that is particularly important for further education. The intention was to minimise learning losses, at least in these areas. Two signals were thus sent – intentionally or not – in terms of educational policy: on the one hand, that not everything that is written into the curriculum for the core subjects is really as important as is always claimed, and on the other hand, that some subjects are quite dispensable.

It is true that some subjects have always found it difficult to be perceived in the discourse on educational policy. Art, music, and sport, for example, fill the margins of the timetables and are the first to be dropped. But the fact that they have been unceremoniously scrapped is a new phenomenon and takes an inhumane educational understanding of school to the extreme. In view of the imbalance in the education system that has become obvious as a result of the Covid-19 pandemic, there is an evident need for urgent curricular reform, on the one hand to declutter and on the other hand to rebalance.

There is a preceding development for all that has become obvious with regard to the curricula as a result of the Covid-19 pandemic. From my point of view, PISA plays an essential role. The decisive factor is not so much the PISA studies themselves, which are of a high standard from an educational science perspective. Rather, it is the reception that PISA has received in educational policy and in the formation of public opinion. This has led to an imbalance in curricula. Their scope has increased rapidly in recent decades. Whereas curricula at the beginning of the twentieth century consisted of only a few pages, today they can quickly reach several hundred. Schools have been assigned more and more tasks. Today, they not only teach reading, arithmetic, and writing but also cope with challenges such as digitalisation and inclusion. However, schools cannot solve all social problems, and students cannot learn an infinite amount. If new things are to be added, others have to be cut from the curricula.

Another problem is that subjects that seem important from a superficial economic point of view receive more attention and support than others. Today, we talk mainly about the STEM subjects, while other subjects are at the subsistence level. Why is less attention paid to the arts, aesthetics, sports, or morals? And why are mathematics, physics, chemistry, and biology an integral part of the subject canon, while education, medicine, or philosophy are not?

At present, the maxim is the earlier, the better. Children are taught all kinds of things as early as preschool age. As sensible as it is to stimulate and support children's development from the very beginning, the question often arises as to how sustainable some support programmes are and whether they address a broad spectrum of abilities and talents. It is not uncommon today for daycare centres to anticipate school. Even if one wants to awaken the spirit of research at an early age, the experiments should be designed in such a way that the children can also understand them.

All this points to a narrow understanding of education. Whether schools lead to social or cultural participation, to peaceful and humane coexistence, to respectful and responsible interaction – all this is given too little attention in the curricula.

Education and educational policy are becoming increasingly global. Thanks to international comparative studies, education is seen as the key to human rights, peace, and prosperity in most countries of the world. However, this development also has a downside: regional characteristics and cultural peculiarities are taking a back seat. Education is not infrequently reduced to the global so that a return to the regional, to an anchoring in the immediate living environment, seems necessary. Global repercussions on the region, from climate change to migration to demographic changes, must be addressed and understood in order to bring about responsible action.

Current curricula do not prepare the young generation for what we already know today – and not for what we cannot know today. They prepare it for what was important yesterday. The coming generation needs not only subject knowledge but also ways of thinking, not only depth in one subject but also the interconnection of subjects, not only expertise but also creativity, not only egocentric striving for achievement but also a respectful and ethical attitude towards one's fellow human beings and the environment.

Therefore, it is time for the following (cf. Nida-Rümelin et al., 2018):

1 The wealth of material in all curricula must be drastically reduced – an old demand that is not wrong just because it is old. The intention in doing so is not to make school easier but more challenging because it is more diverse.
2 The courage to take gaps must be increased – the endeavour to cover a subject comprehensively in school inevitably leads to lazy knowledge.
3 At least 25 per cent of teaching time must be devoted to key problems of our time: social justice, sustainability from an ecological, economic, and social point of view, democratisation, and war and peace – this will make curricula flexible so that they can deal with current challenges appropriately. The Covid-19 pandemic is also an example of this.
4 The region and the homeland must be given greater attention. Concrete projects should start with the question of where the local cultural, political, and historical starting point is and only then build on

this to develop global connections. Recognition of diversity and power of judgement are based on knowledge of one's own identity. "Fridays for Future" is a controversial example of this. It cannot be that the next generation learns more about its future on the street than in school!

5 Education must be decelerated – learning needs time, also and especially in times of digitalisation. If students are to not only learn a subject but also understand it, leisure in a positive sense is indispensable.

6 Humanity must be the guiding principle of the curricula – a further economisation of education must be stopped. It is inhumane to ask about the value of human beings and to reduce education accordingly.

7 Inter- and transdisciplinary thinking must be expanded. For example, the key problem of sustainability cannot be tackled with a sum of physical, biological, chemical, and other knowledge alone, despite the necessity of professionalism. Rather, it requires the reflective and creative use of specialised knowledge and skills across disciplinary boundaries.

8 Practical, creative, and ethical questions for teaching must be rediscovered – the human being is more than what an intelligence test measures.

Last but not least, it is important to point out a bundle of subjects whose potential is still unrecognised today: art, music, and sport. These are the subjects that live particularly on cooperation and collaboration, that encourage and demand creativity, that build on communication, and that consider critical thinking as a basic requirement. Even if the 4C model cited here (collaboration, communication, creativity, critical thinking) is more reminiscent of a technical standard and is often seen as a pseudo-theory of digitalisation euphoria, in the subjects mentioned it finds a fitting culmination. In this respect, the measures to contain Covid-19 are proving to be a wake-up call to place the arts and sports at the centre of future curricula, particularly because educational inequalities are less pronounced and less reinforced in these subjects. On the contrary, these subjects form the social cement that is necessary for a democracy. They are the subjects that best ensure educational justice because they always address the individual in all his or her possibilities and thus have positive effects on mental, physical, and social health.

The core elements of a curricular reform should be a significant reduction in the amount of content, especially in the core subjects, on the one hand, and a stronger emphasis on the mentioned subjects of arts, music, and sports on the other hand. This is required by the Covid-19 pandemic alone because too much teaching time has been lost, and the learning deficits can hardly be compensated. It is important to note that it is not enough to do something only for the year after the Covid-19 pandemic, but that curriculum reform must now be tackled for all grades. This is the only way to achieve educational justice.

The formulated eight points may meet with broad agreement. But when it comes to implementation, opinions will differ: doesn't all this pedagogical wishful thinking lack a connection to reality? Cut at least 25 per cent and do what? In the following, I would like to put this to the test and present the model of modern lesson blocks. It has its roots in reform pedagogy and was also seen by the German educationalist Wolfgang Klafki (1927–2016) as a way of dealing with epochal key problems. As such, he defines challenges for society as a whole, which are red hot, of global significance, have grown historically, and can only be met in an interdisciplinary way. Previous curricula leave no room for this but rather lapse into an 'preambellyrics' that you can often read at the beginning of curricula and in which all the pressing questions of the time are formulated in very general terms but no one feels responsible for them. This makes them seem alien to the lives of children and young people.

In retrospect, the time may not have been ripe for a corresponding reorganisation of everyday school life. In view of the consequences of the Covid-19 pandemic together with the general challenges of our time, modern epochal teaching in lesson blocks is one, if not the most, sustainable approach for the implementation of a curriculum reform. For this purpose, I have taken a look at the timetable for fifth grade at the German gymnasium, which roughly comprises the following subjects and number of hours: mathematics (four), German (native language) (five), English (foreign language) (six), religion (two), geography (two), biology (two), art (two), music (three), and sport (four), with a total of 30 lessons per week.

Step 1: The subjects of arts, music, and sports must be consistently placed at the beginning of the school day. It is unacceptable that these subjects continue to stand on the sidelines of the day and are always the first to fall victim to a shortening of the school day, no matter how responsible this may be. It is precisely the imbalance in physical development that requires a focus on physical learning – also and above all with a view to educational equity.

Step 2: One period of each of the following subjects is diverted and reserved for lesson blocks: mathematics, German, geography, biology, and religion, and even two hours of English. That is eight periods out of 30, or a good 25 per cent.

Step 3: The eight periods thus gained are divided up as follows: the lesson blocks open and close each week in the third period on Monday and Friday, respectively. On Tuesday, Wednesday, and Thursday, the lesson blocks are the third and fourth periods.

Step 4: In the lesson block on Monday, the class discusses a current topic that is to be worked on for at least one week. This topic should be relevant to the students' lives. Appropriate democratic procedures should be used in the beginning as a means of achieving legitimacy among the students. Social learning and the meaning of what has been learned thus become core ideas of the lessons.

Step 5: After the topics have been identified, they are dealt with in the subjects. One thing is clear: interdisciplinary thinking requires disciplinary thinking. In this respect, the subjects, which seem at first to have lost an hour, turn out to play a central role. Thus, a deeper disciplinary exploration of the topic follows in the lesson blocks on Tuesday, Wednesday, and Friday. Mathematics, German, English, and the other subjects, therefore, receive adequate attention but are treated in a way that is more relevant to the students' lifeworld.

Step 6: Finally, the lesson blocks are approached from an interdisciplinary angle on Friday. The findings from the subjects are presented and discussed, negotiated, and weighed up before a decision is finally reached democratically. Once again, social learning and the question of meaning play a decisive role.

The advantages of modern epochal teaching in lesson blocks is obvious: it ensures a connection to the students' lifeworld, creates space for interdisciplinary thinking, demands social learning, implements democratic principles, and provides time for discussion. With this organisational platform, curricular reform can be implemented in the understanding described earlier, thus ensuring that structural measures have an effect right down to the level of interactions in the classrooms.

Empowering people

For all the clarity with which an educational catastrophe resulting from the Covid-19 pandemic has been announced, there are also people who have emerged from the crisis unscathed, some of them even strengthened. What were their preconditions and what can be concluded from this for the future of the education system? In the following, we will look at the most important actors for educational success – namely, learners, parents, and teachers. All of them will show that there are certain factors that should be placed at the centre of reform movements.

Learners: Breaking out of learned passivity

First, let us take a look at the learners: without a doubt, there are learners who were better able to cope with the changed conditions than others during the Covid-19 pandemic, be it social isolation or distance learning. So while some came through the crisis relatively unscathed, others fell off. What can this difference in crisis management be attributed to, and what does it imply for future educational processes, especially in terms of averting the impending educational catastrophe?

A look at distance learning and the conditions necessary for it to work for students provides an interesting perspective. Digital equipment is mentioned too quickly in this context. This is important because without it, distance learning is not possible. But it only lays the foundation. What builds on it is crucial (cf. Zierer, 2020c): virtues such as concentration, perseverance, and commitment are central to distance learning, as is the learners' self-concept, which determines how they handle their own learning. Students who were able to organise their learning, act independently and autonomously, manage and rhythmise their time meaningfully, concentrate, persevere, and remain committed to the task at hand coped better with distance learning than learners who could not and did not do all this. The problem with these factors is that they can generally be influenced by the teacher only to a limited extent – and certainly not in a hurry when schools are closed overnight.

Again and again, they roam the country and win their followers: those who preach that human beings are self-determined beings and that therefore all pedagogical thinking and action must be based exclusively on the learner. Teachers must be learning companions and not teachers, they must be a 'guide on the side' rather than a 'sage on the stage'. What fuels these positions above all is the discussions about digitalisation. Ultimately, people have the opportunity to decide for themselves, with complete freedom, when to learn what, with whom, and why. As euphoric as all this may sound, it fails to recognise the realities of life and runs the risk of becoming utopian.

It is undoubtedly true that human beings, as free beings, have the possibility to free themselves from their constraints and to decide in favour of something. However, it is often overlooked that self-determination is only a gift – and as such, it is a lifelong task that does not come about on its own but requires guided educational processes. The mere possibility of being able to decide for oneself does not force one to choose the right thing. Jürgen Habermas (2019) therefore speaks of 'reasonable freedom'. Two examples.

In preschools and primary schools, it is not uncommon to find the idea that children learn better if they can decide for themselves when to learn. Debates even go so far as to consider giving learners complete freedom as to when to come to class. From the point of view of school organisation alone, this is absurd, but it is also empirically untenable (cf. Hattie et al., 2019). The dumb-and-dumber effect describes what happens in learning arrangements of complete freedom: lower-performing learners often overestimate themselves when choosing their tasks, whereas higher-performing learners tend to underestimate themselves. Learners are only partially able to accurately assess their own performance and therefore need instruction from the teacher.

This effect also applies to universities and colleges, where the overall situation is no better: students today often have complete freedom. They decide when to come and when to go. Attendance lists are frowned upon, usually even forbidden. And exams can often be written as often as needed until the exam is passed or the grade finally fits.

All these effects are the result of a wrongly understood self-determination, which Plato already criticises in his *Politeia*: if the father is afraid of the son and the son plays the father, if teachers are afraid of students and students dictate to teachers what is to be done, in other words, if dependents are just as free as those on whom they are dependent, then freedom degenerates into arbitrariness because there are no longer any limits. But freedom needs boundaries. If in the case of social interaction it is human dignity that functions as the universal limit, in the pedagogical context, it is the responsibility of the older generation towards the younger generation.

This is confirmed by the well-known self-determination theory (cf. Deci et al., 1993), according to which the more autonomous, socially integrated, and challenging the learning situation is, the greater is the motivation to learn. It shows that it is precisely this pedagogically effective framework that is needed for learning to be successful. In Immanuel Kant's words, freedom and coercion are fundamental poles of pedagogy. If they are misjudged or even ignored, it is the end of pedagogy. If this balancing act is not successful, the initial euphoria towards the education system gives way, and friends are soon the only reason to go there, as education researcher Lee Jenkins (2015) shows. The reason to go to school is no longer learning or even education.

Neither self-determination nor foreign determination should be exaggerated and understood as utopias. They require teachers who stand up for values and act as educational agents with the aim of empowering students in all areas of education to be able to make their own decisions sensibly or to be able to use freedom sensibly.

Parents: Encouraging their role in the educational process

Let us now turn to parents: when it comes to the question of educational success and educational equity, it is quickly concluded in public debates that socio-economic status is decisive in this regard. Families with a lot of economic, cultural, and social capital have advantages that benefit their children in a special way. This is the aforementioned Matthew effect. This result has been confirmed empirically many times over. Socio-economic status seems to have a special effect. Education then becomes something that is fixed from the outset, over which the family and also the individual no longer have any influence. The fact that this is not the case is proven time and again by those who have risen up the educational ladder.

In view of the impending educational catastrophe triggered by the Covid-19 pandemic, which has hit educationally disadvantaged milieus particularly hard, it is more important than ever to look into successful families in order to be able to recognise what distinguishes them and, as a result, what needs to be done in terms of educational policy. Against this background, a study by Betty Hart and Todd R. Risley is worth mentioning. It made the headlines in 2003 and is still being discussed today under the heading: "The 30 Million Word Gap". What did Betty Hart and Todd R. Risley research?

For over two years, Betty Hart and Todd R. Risley visited 42 families to study the interactions between children and their parents at home. The families were accompanied once a month for one hour, and the events were observed, recorded, and analysed – in total more than 1,300 hours of data material. The children were between 7 and 9 months old at the beginning of the study and 3 years old at the end. In order to obtain differentiated results with regard to the socio-economic status of the families, they were divided into an upper, a middle, and a lower level, as well as social welfare recipients. The findings are remarkable: Hart and Risley sum up that children as young as three years of age already copy their parents – in the way they talk, walk, play, and even act to take care of a doll. In detail, they conclude that there is a dramatic difference in interaction and dialogue in the families studied and that this is related to socio-economic status. At the age of 3, for example, children differ significantly with regard to their vocabulary: children from a milieu close to education have almost three times as much vocabulary as children from a milieu with little education. This difference does not diminish in the following school years. In this respect, there is no so-called wash-out effect, according to which school and teaching compensate for these differences. On the contrary, the differences not only remain but even increase. Hart and Risley identify the level of linguistic stimulation at home as one reason for these differences in linguistic abilities. Through their observations, they arrive at the following calculation: children from educationally advantaged backgrounds hear about 45 million words by the age of 3, whereas children from educationally disadvantaged backgrounds hear just 15 million words. This results in the gigantic "30 Million Word Gap".

Since quantities are not equal to qualities, Betty Hart and Todd R. Risley also investigated the relationship between linguistic encouragement and linguistic discouragement. Here, too, the result was clear: children from educationally advantaged backgrounds were up to seven times more likely to receive encouragement than discouragement, and children from educationally disadvantaged backgrounds were more than twice as likely to hear discouragement than encouragement.

Betty Hart and Todd R. Risley's conclusion is clear: by the age of 3, a course is set with regard to education that can hardly be made up for later, and if so, only with enormous effort. Consequently, the only solution they see is to strengthen families in cooperation with educational institutions. What could this look like in concrete terms? One example might be parent cafés where parents can get to know other families and teachers, where barriers to contact can be broken down, and where impulses can be given to make parents aware of their role in the educational process. At first glance, this includes such simple things as checking in with the children every day to see how they are doing, showing interest in school, taking a regular look at notebooks, and supporting children when they have concerns. A second look shows that these principles of successful parental involvement are not common in educationally deprived milieus. Parent cafés work best when they are present. But if they are not possible in this way, all avenues of digitalisation must be used. What must no longer be allowed to happen is a loss of contact between school and home. This could be observed many times during the Covid-19 pandemic: parents' meetings were simply cancelled, and teachers no longer offered any consultation hours. Even the telephone hours they then implemented often missed the target. Why? Because parents in educationally disadvantaged milieus do not pick up the phone so easily but see it as an obstacle to communication. This is precisely why it is necessary for teachers to proactively shape parental involvement. The impulses and contacts must come from them if educational equity is to be achieved.

Families, therefore, play a central role in educational success. Strengthening them is not only a top priority in view of the Covid-19 pandemic. However, the crisis has made it particularly clear what happens when contact between school and home breaks down and learners suddenly disappear. The negative consequences then affect the health of children and young people as much as their education.

Teachers: Stop narrowing the focus on subject matter knowledge and put the focus on attitude

Finally, let's look at the teachers: How can they be supported? To answer this question, it is once again worth analysing the Covid-19 pandemic. There were indeed schools that did not lose any learners and reached all of them in the crisis, and there were teachers who successfully implemented their educational mandate even under the most adverse circumstances. What is their secret?

Neither was it solely the structures, the methods, or the media that came into play nor was it the important but not solely effective subject matter knowledge that was the sole guarantor. Rather, successful schools in crisis confirm that the secret of teachers' success lies above all in the way the teaching staff think about school. Researchers speak of collective expectations of effectiveness. What is meant by this? An example will serve to clarify (cf. Hattie et al., 2019).

In 2015, a multi-part documentary about a school development process made headlines: Kambrya College was preparing to go from being one of the worst schools in Australia to one of the best. Founded in 2002 in Brewick, barely 50 kilometres from Melbourne, the school now has over 1,000 students, over 25 per cent of whom have a migrant background, representing over 35 nationalities in total. A typical school in the twenty-first century, if you will. Due to the poor performance of the learners in national comparative tests, the school was declared a so-called red school in 2008. As a result, the school management team around the headmaster Michael Muscat set out and established contacts, among others, with the Graduate School of Education at the University of Melbourne. In this exchange, numerous research findings were taken up to advance the school. After a short time, it was possible to reform the school and put it on the road to success. To cite just one example of a particularly effective measure: all teachers agreed that the objectives would be made visible at the beginning of every lesson, that all methods and media would be explained to the learners, and that the criteria for success would be explained again at the end of the lesson. This consensus alone led to more talking about teaching in the school and also to a real dialogue with the learners finding its way into the lessons. This is because the three previously described aspects were hung up centrally in the classrooms with corresponding word cards.

So if a school succeeds in developing a common vision of education, in defining criteria for teaching quality and using them as a daily guideline, it can achieve a lot even in a crisis. At the centre of this thinking is not the question: do we have enough tablets? But rather the pedagogical question par excellence: who is the human being? If you want to get through the crisis successfully from a pedagogical point of view and, above all, learn from the crisis, you have to give schools space and time to formulate a collective expectation of effectiveness for themselves. This certainly requires teacher training and further education, which, unlike in the past, should not be one-day events but rather longer-term programmes that are not attended by individuals but address the entire teaching staff, put mistakes at the centre of the exchange about school and teaching, and finally lead from lone warriors to team players. This does not mean that everyone has to do the same thing from now on. Rather, the crucial point is to work together on a vision of education and school. If teachers teach an average of 35,000 lessons in the course of their lives and none of these lessons is perfect, then it is high time to use this potential for error to promote a professionalisation offensive as a team.

The role of school leadership becomes visible in this context – it is therefore high time for its training to finally receive a systematic and scientific foundation. After all, the task of school leadership is to develop a cooperative climate in the teaching staff, to implement rules and rituals of cooperation, and to provide appropriate framework conditions.

What does this mean for teacher education in the future? In view of the shortage of teachers, it is certainly to be welcomed that more people are studying to become teachers. But quality must not be forgotten. If, for example, the German state Bavaria has several thousand students for every school education professorship, then that is an unacceptable starting situation. Just for comparison: in the course of the governmental digitalisation offensive, 1,000 professorships will be created for 10,000 students in Bavaria – a ratio of 1:10! A dream for research and teaching. School education is miles away from this. What kind of signal is this sending to teachers? A look at France makes one envious: after the murder of a teacher, the head of state made visible the importance of teachers for democracy in a speech at the Sorbonne. Pars pro toto, a quote from Emmanuel Macron: "We all carry in our hearts and memories the image of a teacher who changed the course of our lives".

This quote sums up the whole importance of teacher professionalism and thus of teacher education. More than ever, we need teachers who do not just teach a subject but people, who are not content with imparting knowledge or even generating competencies. Because that is not the core of education. Education is not what I have been made into but what I have made of my life. We need teachers who stand behind what they teach, who are committed to democracy and above all to humanity, who do not make young people parrot back information but make them think. We need teachers who do not only have a high level of subject matter knowledge, pedagogical, and didactic competence but also a high level of heart and character building. Without all this, we will not succeed in overcoming the current challenges – whether it is climate change, the Covid crisis, or the recurring refugee issue. For these challenges have a moral core at their centre.

Not everything that would be necessary for this with regard to teacher education is new, but that does not mean that it is outdated. I formulate four theses (cf. Zierer, 2021e):

> First, it is important to create structures that empower people. We need reasonable framework conditions that enable exchange, cooperation, and reflection. It is possible to pass on knowledge at a mass event with over 1,300 students (what I have to do every semester in Augsburg, Germany) – with the help of digital media, it can even be done for several thousand. But when it comes to professionalisation, this mass exceeds the limits of what is pedagogically feasible. Consequently, the educational science aspect of teacher education must be expanded and given more personnel. In the context of this expansion, the relationship between theory and practice must also be discussed. It must not, as often happens, be simply about more practice. We know from research that students can spend months on an internship. If this is not reflected upon in an appropriate

framework, the learning success is zero – at best, because it can also be negative. So what we need is a stronger dovetailing of theory and practice. Theory without practice is empty, as is practice without theory. This raises the question of whether teacher training in which there are three isolated phases is and ever was a wise idea: the first phase, university studies, is dominated by theory, while practice is neglected. In the second phase, the traineeship, it is the other way around. Practice dominates and theory is dismissed with the words: "Now forget everything you learned at university". In the third phase, after the attainment of a permanent position, it often becomes a matter of self-teaching: everyone does what they want, while quite a few do nothing. From this perspective, the existing teacher education system shows itself to be an ailing institution that needs to be thoroughly reformed. A coherent interlocking and interaction of theory and practice is a central demand.

Second, it is important to focus on the teacher. Teachers are agents of education. Their task is not to impart mere knowledge. Likewise, their task is not to be merely the facilitator of learning processes. It is about education, and thus about people with their possibilities, but also their limitations. Raising awareness for this is the central task of future teacher education. This requires more than providing teachers with a lot of subject matter knowledge. A high degree of pedagogical and didactic competence is also needed. And as a basis for all three together, a professional attitude is necessary, which should run like a thread through the individual phases of teacher education. The teaching profession is not only a profession; it is also a vocation. It is always about normative questions, about values, about ethical decisions. Not only are knowledge and skills required, but also heart and character – this applies to the learners but also and above all to the teachers. The greatest effect that teachers have on their students does not result from the fact that they teach a certain subject and are particularly competent in it, or that they are particularly good with new media, or that they are particularly humorous. The greatest effect comes when they perceive students as people, and thus appear as someone who believes in learners, helps them, and stands by their side even when things get difficult. The basis for this is a clear understanding of education, a vision of what our world should look like not only today but also tomorrow. Without this debate on values, no education is possible – and it must be moved to the centre of teacher education. If the measure of all things at universities continues to be the amount of third-party funding and citation indices, the university mission of teacher education will not be realised.

Third, we need team players instead of lone warriors. Teacher education has long been, and in many cases still is today, a lone wolf approach. Young teachers are socialised at an early age to stand alone in front of the class and meet all the challenges themselves. The classic teaching exams are taken alone – and so, thousands of exam hours are reinvented again and again every year. This understanding of the profession does not do justice to global challenges: compared to the past, social developments today have not only become more complex but also faster. More than ever, team spirit is required. Against this background, what numerous studies demonstrate fits into the picture: teacher professionalism develops best in a culture of cooperation where mistakes are welcome and where they are worked on together. In future, teacher education must demand and promote this team spirit more strongly than before. Teaching and examination concepts that foster this cooperation must be implemented already at universities. Schools need to add examination formats which focus not only on individual performance but also on teamwork, not only on error-free lessons but also on how mistakes are dealt with in lessons – there is no lesson in which everything runs perfectly. And finally, as lifelong learning, the teaching profession always needs an attitude that is characterised by exchange and cooperation. Let's put up a board in teaching staff rooms titled "The Mistake of the Week" and use our mistakes to drive our teacher professionalism!

Fourth, evidence must come before fashions. Hardly any other social field is subject to as many fashions as schools – and unfortunately also to as many myths. Yesterday it was architectural gimmicks, today it is digital media that are used to promise educational revolutions. In most cases, however, we have to recognise that these revolutions do not exist. Empirical studies provide evidence that certain basic principles of learning and teaching endure: learning needs a positive teacher–student relationship, a good culture of error, goals that are not too easy but also not too difficult to achieve, phases of practice and consolidation, and commitment and effort in all educational paths, which do not always run in a straight line but repeatedly turn out to be detours and wrong turns.

Without these basic principles, any innovations in the field of education quickly become a flash in the pan – and many a potential dies with them. For example, anyone who believes today that classroom management can be trained in a virtual space may be moving with the times, but they have still not understood the basic principles of learning and teaching. Because research shows: people need people – also in teacher training.

In view of all these considerations, teachers who stand behind their educational mission are needed more than ever. More than ever, we need to focus on people instead of always putting economic interests in the foreground of education. In this way, it is possible to avert an impending educational catastrophe and to ensure more educational justice in the future.

Professionalising teaching

Perhaps one of the most positive side effects of the Covid-19 pandemic has been the unprecedented rethinking of good teaching. After all, school closures, hygiene-restricted teaching, distance learning, or even learning in rotation were new territory for everyone involved, and so everyone had to set out on their own. This momentum must be carried forward if we want to avert the impending educational catastrophe. For despite the importance of structural measures, it is the quality within the structures that determines whether learning is successful.

The truth at this point is that it was possible to avoid the challenge outlined earlier. Some teachers were submerged during the first lockdown. In the second lockdown, it was no longer possible to do so because regulations had been introduced and the technical conditions were also in place. However, this alone was no guarantee for good teaching. Many children and young people had to spend several hours a day in front of screens and endure endless monologues. In the classrooms, the 'hands – face – space rules' not infrequently led to a lot of teaching time falling victim to hygiene measures and the lessons themselves degenerating into the worst frontal teaching ever.

Teachers who thought through the intended scenarios of the lessons pedagogically from the very beginning acted quite differently. They were the ones who taught successfully and did not lose any students. For them, the guiding questions were always, What is good teaching under the given circumstances, and what can I do as a teacher to ensure that all students can achieve the best possible learning success? Empirical educational research has formulated answers to these questions, which unfortunately have not yet been comprehensively adopted in everyday school practice. In addition, educational policy has not managed to come up with a pedagogical master plan during the Covid-19 pandemic to date. Just as scientific findings were listened to in the fight against the Covid-19 pandemic, it is high time for myths and fashions to be separated from truths and findings in the education system as well.

Ensuring teaching quality

The question of how to capture teaching quality in a few words has always preoccupied empirical educational research and has been translated into a number of models for measuring teaching quality (cf. Brophy, 1999; Meyer, 2004; MET, 2010; Helmke, 2014). As different as these models appear at first glance, it can nevertheless be stated that the similarities are greater than the differences. This is reassuring and important for teachers because the conclusion is that it is not decisive which model of teaching quality is ultimately followed. It is more important that evidence be the basis for decisions in teaching practice. Because this ensures that empirical results provide the framing for education and teaching.

The following presentation of the 7 Cs (cf. MET, 2010) is intended to bring a viable model for teaching quality into the discussion for the future. This can be helpful for any scenario in the Covid-19 pandemic – whether face-to-face with hygiene requirements, distance learning, or hybrid teaching – but also afterwards. And it provides the basis for teaching to achieve the goal of reducing educational inequalities and enabling more educational equity:

1 Care: Learning needs an atmosphere of trust and confidence. Without positive relationships between the learners and the teacher, but also between the learners themselves, many efforts will be ineffective.
2 Control: Research on learning success confirms again and again how important the factor 'classroom management' is. It is the guarantee that learning takes place smoothly and with momentum, without distractions, and in social interaction.
3 Challenge: Learning must be neither too easy nor too difficult. If one leads to under-challenging, over-challenging is the consequence of the other. Both cases significantly reduce learning success. Instead, it is the challenge in learning that counts. This is achieved above all by ensuring that the tasks to be completed are only just manageable for learners.
4 Clarify: The clearer the goals learners are expected to achieve and the more clearly learners are made aware of what learning success should look like, the more successful they will be in learning.
5 Confer: Learning is a social process. Even in phases of learning alone, one is only alone at first glance. A second look shows that the video, the book, the worksheet, and so on are the work of an other and thus have social character. But that's not all: as long as school is about education, social interactions play the crucial role. For it is only in exchange with each other that one questions oneself, reconsiders one's values and norms, applies the acquired knowledge in everyday life, and thus further develops one's personality.
6 Captivate: Learning is not possible without motivation. It is known from research that there are different forms of motivation: on the one hand, there is extrinsic motivation, which is quite effective, but also very short-lived. Students learn in these situations not because they are interested in the subject matter but because they are offered a motive

from outside. Often it is even the peers, that is, those of the same age, who motivate learners. On the other hand, there is intrinsic motivation, which is just as effective but has the advantage of having a lasting effect. So students learn in these situations mainly because they are interested in the subject.

7 Consolidate: Determining whether learners have achieved the objectives is indispensable from a didactic point of view. Not only do teachers need this information to plan the next lesson, but it is also important for learners to know what they have achieved and what they need to work on next.

A didactic approach that is particularly well suited to implementing what has been said and is all the more important against the backdrop of an impending educational catastrophe is the so-called learning path. These essentially mean that learners are presented on the basis of intelligent diagnostics with a sequence of tasks that, depending on their level of achievement, are not too easy and not too difficult but always within the area of challenge. In each subject, for example, three performance levels can be defined for each learning objective: lower, intermediate, and higher. At each of these performance levels, it is possible to formulate a sequence of several tasks that successively build on each other, thus clarifying the transition from one performance level to the next. A learning path now shows the learner at which level he or she is located and which tasks he or she has to work on next in order to progress one step further.

A prerequisite for moving on in the task sequence is the successful completion of the preceding tasks. If too many mistakes are made, further practice steps must be taken and, under certain circumstances, further help must be offered through explanations by tutors, teachers, or digital media. A learning path is thus not a rigid grid but adapts to the learning progress of the students. Through the integration of digital media, especially in the central phases of diagnosis, implementation, and evaluation, a targeted and transparent approach to the learning process is possible. Learners are always aware of the next steps, parents can track strengths and weaknesses, and teachers have time for the most important processes in learning: building relationships, giving and receiving feedback, setting impulses, and using mistakes as an opportunity for discussion. This shows that learning pathways implement all the criteria of successful teaching mentioned earlier: by taking into account the learning requirements and time windows for exchange, they help to build an atmosphere of trust and confidence (care). A clear sequence of tasks gives orientation and security (control). Since the tasks in the learning path are always assigned in relation to the learner's performance level, challenge is guaranteed (challenge). Furthermore, the learning path makes a sequence of tasks and thus also the learning success visible to the students in the presentation of performance levels and corresponding learning tasks (clarify). Learning motivation can thus be established, because, first, work is always done in the area of challenge, and, second, work is always done with a goal in mind (captivate). By consciously giving and receiving feedback, learners not only receive indications of how they are progressing in the learning process (consolidate), but they are also given the opportunity to help shape their learning process (confer).

In view of the possibilities and the empirically proven effectiveness of learning pathways, for example within the framework of the 'response to intervention' approach, it is surprising that they are not yet part of the school system. Digital media in particular offer a variety of possibilities for providing such learning pathways effectively and for many learners at the same time so that even beyond the Covid-19 pandemic, they represent an important element for bringing individual support into everyday school life. In the challenge of overcoming the crisis, however, they represent the means of choice – and in this respect, the one billion euros from the German federal government for the aforementioned tutoring programme is an opportunity to implement a didactic approach which is long overdue on a broad scale.

Making digitalisation pedagogical

The example of learning pathways has made it clear that digitalisation has great potential in the education sector – especially when it comes to individual support and thus more educational equity. Without a doubt, the measures to contain Covid have led to a digitalisation push in the school context. For various reasons, this should initially be seen as positive. The most obvious reason is certainly that without digital media, no schooling would have been possible during the lockdown. Another good thing about this digitalisation push is that some countries have finally caught up with other countries in terms of equipping schools with digital media (cf. ICILS 2018). Even if country comparisons are always short-sighted, there is no question that the lifeworld of children, young people, and adults is shaped by digital media – and will be even more so in the future than it is today. In this respect, it makes no sense from an educational point of view to discuss whether digital media should be covered in school or not. School has to face the challenge that the digitalisation of society brings with it. Furthermore, the good thing about this digitalisation push is that it removes any possible excuses from the table for a long time. Today, no one can say that they would like to use digital media in the classroom but that the possibilities are simply not there yet. Both the money and the hardware and software are now available in such a variety that the possibilities increase from day to day. This, however, poses the real challenge of digitalisation, which has often fallen by the wayside due to the speed of decision-making in the wake of the Covid-19 pandemic: technology is neither the bringer of salvation nor devil's stuff, neither only good for people nor only bad for them.

The consequence of this was and still is a division of the discourse into two camps (cf., for the following, Nida-Rümelin et al., 2020): on the one hand those who fear the demise of occidental educational traditions with the arrival of tablets, laptops, and other technical devices and on the other hand those who see the opportunity coming in times of digital transformation to throw everything overboard that has developed over centuries of educational knowledge. The doomsayers of digital media are accused of cultivating defensive reflexes and refusing to embrace the new worlds of learning, while conversely, the advocates of a far-reaching digital transformation of everyday education are caricatured as propagandists of an ever-advancing economisation of general education.

In order to be able to outline this future task, it is necessary to distinguish between two perspectives that have been ignored for years in the debate on a digitalisation of the education sector:

First, consider the perspective of education and the related question: "What are the consequences of digitalisation for education?" In a humanistic understanding, education shows itself in what I have made of my life and not in what one has made of me. Thus, the human being with all his or her possibilities is always at the centre of education. The human being as the author of his or her life becomes the focal point of education. The digital transformation is changing the forms and structures of communication and interaction, of information and decision-making. The availability of data is growing exponentially, while its theoretical but also its lifeworld interpretation, classification, and evaluation are changing only gradually. Digitalisation in the field of education must therefore be aimed above all at counteracting this drifting apart of exponentially growing pools of data on the one hand and cognitive overload on the other. The old – humanistic – educational ideal of judgement is therefore the central goal of education. It must be directed towards overcoming the parcelling of knowledge in school lessons, making connections clear, and promoting critical faculties. This requires spaces for reflection and distance, which cannot be provided without curricular reform.

In view of a generation of young people who have grown up with digital devices and developed a high degree of skill in their use, it cannot be the goal of school to double or triple the time students spend each day in front of displays, which is already at the limit of what is pedagogically acceptable. Young people can already operate the devices – they understand digital technology. What they don't understand is the insidious processes that unthinking media consumption sets in motion. For example, a large number of research studies show that the amount of time spent using the internet is directly and negatively related to cognitive performance – with children and young people from educationally deprived backgrounds being particularly disadvantaged. Studies also show that extensive and skilled use of technology does not result in a deeper understanding of software architectures and algorithms. This requires at least rudimentary knowledge of a programming language, the communication mechanisms in social media, and the potential of digital innovation in commerce and industry. An essential goal of digitalisation in education must be to familiarise children and young people with these mechanisms and to make them immune to the trend towards ideologisation, ideological standardisation, and the compartmentalisation of conflicting views; in other words, to empower them to become independent actors in the digital worlds of communication and interaction. This is especially important against the backdrop of educational inequalities, which open the door to manipulation, dependency, and radicalisation.

Second, consider the perspective of teaching and the related question: "How can the use of digital media optimise learning processes?" A look at the results of empirical educational research shows (cf. Zierer, 2019) that digital media have only moderate effects on learning success. The core message is thus clear: digitalisation is not an end in itself. Rather, we need an evidence-based didactics that makes visible where the possibilities and limits of digital media lie. Digitalisation in education must not lead to a disempowerment of the teacher, because according to all empirical studies, it is not the age of the learners, not the subject, not a particular medium, but the personal bond between teacher and learners that is of central importance for learning success and ultimately also for educational success. Whether it is the laptop or the tablet that learners use, the PowerPoint that teachers use, or even such comprehensive didactic approaches as the flipped classroom, which creates more time for communication in class by shifting the input to the preparation phase – empirical evidence always points to the fact that it is people who bring technology to life by integrating digital media into the classroom in a meaningful – that is, pedagogically reflected and didactically skilful – way. These findings of empirical educational research are systematically ignored by industry because everything that is technically possible is realised. A series of innovations can be found under the heading 'learning analytics' that seem interesting at first glance but reveal at second glance that people are to be replaced by machines and, by extension, that people are even to be treated like machines.

Even if a cold computer can in some cases be more effective for learning than an incompetent pedagogue, if it is not only about learning but about education, then humans need humans. Thus, some digital tools lead in everyday school life to isolation and withdrawal, a tendency already shown by excessive use of social media and gaming, with sometimes highly problematic cultural and social consequences – precisely because they have a stronger effect on children and young people from educationally deprived milieus. The Summit Learning Project, which is being implemented by Mark Zuckerberg and his wife Priscilla Chan, a paediatrician, at almost 400 schools in the USA, is a noteworthy example in this context (cf. Nida-Rümelin et al., 2020). At the centre is a personalised learning platform that is intended to enable individual learning and thus targeted support. The learning platform adapts examination questions, learning objectives, and tasks to the individual student. The teacher thus becomes a mentor who accompanies the students as they learn separately from each other. However, it turns out that several schools have already left the Summit programme because parents and their children complained about the hours of screen time. The learners lacked interaction and direct communication and felt isolated. This was compounded by physical ailments such as hand discomfort due to hours of computer work. The poor quality of the websites used as information sources also received harsh criticism – the content was not easily accessible without a teacher, often poorly articulated, with advertising links and banners, and often of a low standard.

Such experiences should not be dismissed as propaganda of the diehards but should be taken seriously. They show that an ill-considered form of digitalisation in education achieves the opposite of what was intended: not a strengthening but a weakening of children and young people, a loss of the teacher–student relationship, a further step towards social isolation and digital dependency. In times of a digitalisation of society, it is thus more important than ever to advance the professionalisation of teachers. They must have the power of judgement to decide which medium to use for which students, when, how, and above all why.

I would like to use 'the grammar of learning' that has evolved with the development of homo sapiens as an example to illustrate what has been said using five principles. This grammar of learning applies regardless of whether analogue or digital media are used for learning. It must therefore be seen as a guiding principle for the digitalisation of teaching (cf. Zierer, 2019).

First, learning requires effort and commitment: Again and again, the thesis is put forward that learning is completely changed by digitalisation. This can be refuted by reference to a central grammar of learning, which can be illustrated with the help of the forgetting curve (cf. Ebbinghaus, 1885). We know from numerous psychological studies that people need around six to eight repetitions to transfer information from short-term memory to long-term memory. If these repetitions and the associated effort and commitment are missing, forgetting takes its course. The moment of forgetting therefore begins at the moment of remembering. And this is independent of whether learning was analogue or digital.

Second, learning requires challenges: It is one of the most consistent messages from tech companies that digitalisation makes learning easier. As nice as this claim sounds, it is wrong: education in general and learning in particular is not easy because it progresses via detours and wrong paths, not infrequently leading to failure and mistakes. In this respect, education must not be about making learning as easy as possible. It must be about making learning as challenging as possible. The flow experience is the best empirical evidence for this grammar of learning (cf. Csíkszentmihályi, 2010): people reach a state of deep satisfaction when they pursue a task that challenges them and where the probability of success is as great as the probability of failure. If digitalisation is to be effective in education, it must be used in such a way that the challenge can be set even better thanks to it than without it.

Third, learning requires positive relationships: It is one of the central findings of anthropology that human beings need a counterpart in order to know themselves. Accordingly, Martin Buber (1958) states, "The human being becomes the I at the You". If this counterpart is missing, one is like Robinson Crusoe: lonely and abandoned, one becomes a stranger to oneself and loses oneself in a world without support and orientation. This finding has been empirically proven many times, for example with the dumb-and-dumber effect (cf. Hattie et al., 2019): People tend to overestimate or underestimate their possibilities. Only rarely does the image one paints of oneself hit the mark. The assessment of others is important. In this respect, the talk – fuelled by digitalisation – of learning guides and excessive individualised learning is not very helpful, but rather nonsensical: learners do not only need a 'guide on the side'. They also need a 'change agent' in every phase of their lives: a person who holds up a mirror to them, who encourages them and challenges them when they do not believe in themselves, but who also puts the brakes on them when they set false expectations.

Fourth, learning requires motivation: The classic discussion about the added benefit of digitalisation in education is the thesis that the use of tablets, smartphones, and the like increases motivation to learn. Empirically, this can be nicely illustrated and confirmed at first glance. However, a second look shows that this increase in motivation decreases again after two to four weeks – at the latest when learners realise that it is all about learning. And so this digitalisation argument suffers from ignorance of the grammar of learning, of the fact that learning requires motivation: but in essence and in the long run, not a motivation that lies outside of learning, but one that is directed towards the thing to be learned.

Fifth, learning requires surface understanding in order to develop deep understanding: In times of Alexa and Siri, it may be indisputable to many that thanks to digitalisation people no longer need factual knowledge: knowledge is available anytime and anywhere, so learners can concentrate all their effort on competency development. This argumentation fails to recognise the difference between factual knowledge and wisdom, as well as the connection between surface understanding and deep understanding, as it has always been known in didactics. In order for learners to enter the realm of deep understanding, which is the goal of education as meaningful and creative thinking oriented toward solving problems, they must have acquired a certain amount of reproducible knowledge. Simply knowing where something is and where to find a piece of information is not enough. Deep understanding is based on surface understanding. And for learners to be able to process this, the facts must be in their heads, not on computers.

Many more such principles of learning could be cited, but the core message is already visible: as long as we are human beings, learning will remain learning. Digitalisation will not change this.

Digitalisation in education is not an alternative to humanistically guided pedagogical practice, but its continuation, indeed its radicalisation. The focus must be on the personal development of children and young people, their power of judgement, their strength of decision, and their thirst for action. Digitalisation in education must also be directed towards creating the conditions for people to be authors of their own lives. In this respect, the goal is not a digital school but rather a humane school in the age of digitalisation. Understood in this way, digitalisation can make a significant contribution to reducing educational inequalities and enabling more educational justice.

Finally, I would like to present an example of digitalisation that takes into account both the perspective of education and the perspective of teaching and thus outlines a way of what a humane school can look like in the age of digitisation. The 7 Cs of teaching quality mentioned at the beginning of this chapter are taken into account as well as the media-pedagogical considerations just mentioned. It is the so-called SAMR model by Ruben R. Puentedura (2021).

As always, there are critics of this model, which are important (cf. Hamilton et al., 2016). In my view, however, it currently represents one of the most convincing models for the use of digitalisation in education in terms of theoretical foundation and empirical verification. The acronym SAMR stands for four levels of the use of digital media (cf. Zierer, 2019).

At the first level, 'substitution', digital media are used to replace traditional media. For example, learners usually have to write an essay with paper and pencil. They can do the same thanks to digital media using a computer or a tablet. The effect on the quality of the story is small because the central aspect of digitalisation – namely, bridging space and time and connecting people – is not used. It is and remains the individual learner who alone fulfils his or her task, and the only thing that has an influence on the essay is that he or she perhaps types faster than by hand.

At the second level, 'augmentation', digital media are used to pick up several traditional media at once. To continue the given example, the learner is not only provided with paper and pencil but also with dictionaries for spelling and grammar, as well as more in-depth factual encyclopaedias. Since all of this is also possible digitally, usually even with a device, there is an expansion that is definitely faster and easier digitally than with traditional media. But here, too, the effect remains small because the central aspect of digitalisation is still not being used. So it is still the individual learners who are alone with their task.

From an empirical point of view, it is not surprising against this background that the levels of replacement and enhancement hardly lead to an improvement in the quality of teaching. The focus is limited, and the possibilities of digitalisation are not yet used. Too often, a traditional medium is replaced with a digital medium: the computer as a lexicon substitute, the beamer as a blackboard substitute, and the tablet as a worksheet substitute. As long as schools remain at these levels, the potential of digitalisation in education will not be able to unfold, but rather various pitfalls will have to be reckoned with. Unused language labs as well as neverending teacher lectures with overloaded presentation slides are deterrent examples of unreflective media use yesterday and today. As a result, the further levels are crucial.

At the third level, 'modification', digital media are used to change the task in a way that would be difficult with traditional media. For example, in the case of the essay, the task is no longer for an individual learner to write it but for learners to come together in a team and produce the text jointly with the help of digital media. Of course, learners can also write a text together with paper and pencil, but digitalisation facilitates this process at the working level and thus creates spaces for creativity and collaboration. When the learners are able to collaborate with learners from other schools or even with experts, such as authors, who are not at the school, this level of change makes it possible to bridge space and time and connect people. The essay will now take on a completely new form that individual learners cannot manage on their own.

At the fourth level, 'redefinition', digital media are used to formulate the task in a way that is not possible with traditional media. In the example presented, the task could be not only to write an essay but also to develop it further into a screenplay and also to film it. This requires not only further occasions for writing in the team but also a new form of implementation which, in addition to the subject matter, allows the digital media themselves to become the learning object. For example, the learners have to decide in shooting the film when to incorporate a change of perspective, which music to use, which narrative format to choose, and so on. All in all, this level uses the possibilities of digitalisation: space and time are bridged and people are connected.

From an empirical point of view, the levels of change and reassignment not only lead to greater learning effects in the subject but also to extensive media education. Thus, they are the ones that both focus on the quality of teaching and take into account the perspectives of teaching and education.

This is especially important for children and young people from educationally deprived milieus because they are demonstrably more affected by possible disadvantages of digitalisation. In this sense, media education is an important field for more educational justice. Understood in this way, digitalisation can make an important contribution to rethinking schools and taking them out of a passive role. Changes in society as a whole always require schools to play an active role because they have to prepare the next generation for the society of today and tomorrow.

4   Rethinking school: Principles of education after Covid

Before I conclude by presenting a catalogue of demands in five principles for rethinking school, I would first like to address three points that became particularly evident as weaknesses of the education system during the Covid-19 pandemic: first, schools have for too long taught a one-sided understanding of education because it is oriented towards just a few cognitive elements. There is a need to rethink and redefine education. Second, in recent, years schools have been reduced to thinking in terms of effectiveness. As important as effectiveness is, it must not be the only factor in the educational process. Education must always be understood as free of purpose if it is not to become a means to an end. And third, this reveals joy to be the elixir of education par excellence. Unfortunately, as empirical studies show, joy in schools is not at its best. In this respect, it is time to make it the guiding principle for education and teaching.

Preparing schools for epochal challenges: less PISA, more education

The discussion on education is moving forward. In the process, the results from PISA are also being criticised. On 6 May 2014, a large group initiated by renowned US educationalists wrote an open letter on the website of *The Guardian* calling on those responsible for PISA to stop the 'PISA mania' and to think differently about education. The accusations are not new, but this time, they are being made prominently and widely: PISA leads to a reduced understanding of education in which the focus is limited to only a small part of what constitutes education. The measuring instruments used are more than questionable and show major weaknesses. The concept of human capital behind PISA turns out to be deeply inhumane when analysed closely. This criticism can be found in the debate under the headings 'economisation of education' or 'instrumentalisation of education'. The danger behind this can be described with the term 'optimisation trap', following Julian Nida-Rümelin (2011): a striving for constant maximisation and increased effectiveness in the education

DOI: 10.4324/9781003408864-4

system leads to shortcuts and undesirable developments. The example of China, one of the PISA winners, can be used to illustrate this: Chinese education is highly effective, and Chinese students are among the best when it comes to mathematical, scientific, and linguistic skills. However, China has one of the highest burnout rates among students and the highest suicide rate in primary education. In short, a growth economy in the field of education leads to educational collapse.

Humanity today faces global challenges. They involve problems that humanity itself has caused and that can only be tackled through global thinking in local contexts of action. Following Wolfgang Klafki (1995), we can speak of epochal challenges. The characteristic features of this type of problem are the following:

- They are of global significance and therefore require global solutions. No nation-state can cope with epochal challenges on its own.
- They have grown historically and come to the fore at a certain time. No nation-state can avoid epochal challenges.
- They have an interdisciplinary character and cannot be viewed from only one perspective. Epochal challenges have at least one economic, ecological, and social facet.
- They require not only a factual analysis but also an ethical one. Consequently, overcoming epochal challenges requires different methodological approaches.

If one takes this characterisation seriously and tries to derive a modern understanding of education from it, then the approach suggested by Howard Gardner (2009) seems important. He developed a programme for the future and speaks of "five minds for the future":

1 People today and in the future need more than just subject knowledge. The core pedagogical idea of a school subject lies not in detailed knowledge but in the way of thinking, in orientation knowledge, in its contribution to self-understanding and understanding of the world. A narrow focus on memorising superficial factual knowledge squanders the possibilities of a subject as well as human potential and makes learning meaningless.
2 People today and in the future must be able to filter out what is most important from the multitude of information, to reflect critically, and to connect it. Subject teaching that is strictly related only to the respective subject and its way of thinking leads to a segmentation of knowledge and prevents inter- and transdisciplinary thinking. This, however, is essential for life in a humane global society.
3 People today and in the future have to be creative if they want to cope with the unpredictable and survive in competition. They must be able

to combine perspectives and work in diverse teams. Expertise in the sense of isolated technical specialisation is becoming less and less important and is no longer in keeping with the times.

4   People today and in the future must have respect for diversity. No one person knows everything and no one person is always right. Acknowledgement of diversity and power of judgement is the basis for democracy and humanity.

5   People today and in the future need an ethical awareness – in all areas of life, for example in religious questions, in cultural questions, and in political questions. All situations in life require not only knowledge and ability but also willingness and values. The ethical dimension of life is required on a large and small scale.

The current and future challenges of society do not require further specialisation in a few competencies or further concentration in a selection of subjects. What is important, besides professionalism, is interdisciplinarity, a respectful and ethical attitude towards one's fellow human beings and the environment, and an egocentric striving for achievement. If this succeeds, pathologies of education are avoided, and at the same time, education can become a motor for social change.

Approaches to answering the central question: what is a good school?

Humanity has the potential to improve the world. However, for this to happen, it needs judgement and drive. In short, it needs education! In view of the numerous processes of change, the current school system seems to have reached its limits. It needs to be rethought.

Often, the first thought in the renewal of the school system is directed at the structures. As important as these are, the decisive effect does not come from them, which is why John Hattie (2015) also calls such debates the "politics of distraction". By this he means that educational policy is limited to the visible facets of a school system while forgetting the invisible ones.

So what is a good school and how can it be recognised, if not by certain structures? To answer this question, I would like to refer to an epistemological model by Ken Wilber (1987), which he developed on the basis of ideas by Karl Popper and Jürgen Habermas. Wilber's core statement is that complex phenomena can be viewed from different perspectives and that each of these perspectives is important in its own right.

Essentially, four epistemological approaches can be distinguished: one objective, one subjective, one intersubjective, and one interobjective. How do these approaches help answer our key question: what is a good school?

Objective approach: From this point of view, empirical methods dominate and knowledge is gained through measuring, testing, and the like. An example of a corresponding statement would be, "It is raining outside". Any person can check this statement quickly and easily. This makes it clear that statements from this point of view claim to be true. When it comes to measuring and testing in the context of school, effectiveness is the defining criterion, and the question of a good school comes down to the sub-question: what is an effective school? Prime examples of this are international comparative studies like PISA, in which the performance of education systems is measured through comparison of countries on the basis of mathematical, scientific, and linguistic competencies. The Visible Learning study (cf. Zierer, 2021a), which has already been cited several times, is also a veritable treasure trove for thinking about the effectiveness of learning and teaching. However, education and school performance are not limited to the competencies mentioned. Let us recall again Howard Gardner's (1983) multiple intelligences: there are also motor, social, affective, moral, ethical, and religious competencies. They are also within the scope of education and teaching but are seldom measured empirically because these competencies elude appropriate measurement. Empirical educational research primarily measures what can be measured well. This is the advantage, but also the disadvantage.

Subjective approach: This perspective is primarily about needs, interests, and feelings. An example of this would be the answer "I'm fine" to the question "How are you?" It is obvious that the truth of this statement is not subject to an empirical approach: it is not possible to check with the help of measurements or tests whether someone is telling the truth or possibly lying. Consequently, statements from this perspective cannot claim truth for themselves but a truthfulness. If one transfers this thought to the question of a good school, the limitation of an objective approach can be made visible: education does not only consist of competencies, and school is not exhausted in being as effective as possible. Equally important are the interests, wishes, and needs of all those involved. Seen from this perspective, the question of a good school thus comes down to the sub-question: what is a joyful school? It is no secret that effective time does not always have to be fulfilled and equally that fulfilled time is not always used effectively. However, both belong to education. The fact that the joy perspective is forgotten in the discussion has to do with an overemphasis on effectiveness.

Intersubjective approach: Values and norms, rules, and rituals play a major role from this perspective, and they have an influence on how people think and act. They can neither be determined empirically nor set by the individual. Rather, they require argumentative and discursive debate. In this respect, the claim that can be made with statements from this perspective is not truth or veracity. Instead, it is about a cultural fit. If one transfers this thought to the question of a good school, the following sub-question can be formulated: what is a culturally appropriate school? In this sense, what is meant is primarily questions of goals and content. These can neither be determined empirically nor can they be determined by the individual. The question of what should be learned in school and why must be answered discursively and argumentatively. Every culture must ask itself these questions. The concept of education must therefore also be constantly redefined. What is considered important today may be outdated tomorrow. One can think, for example, of environmental education, which received special attention with the nuclear disaster in Chernobyl in 1986, only to fade into the background again for several years. Recent headlines on climate change bring this topic back to the top of the agenda.

Interobjective approach: Systemic perspectives dominate here, according to which no human being exists alone but is integrated into various contexts – into the family, the economy, politics, and the church, to name perhaps the most important at this point. According to Niklas Luhmann's systems theory, which can be associated with this perspective, there are numerous tensions between the individual systems. These are mainly due to the different codes with which the systems express themselves and work: politics is primarily concerned with power, business with profits, the church with faith, schools with education, and so on. These different interests can lead to conflicts and controversies. Their clarification requires statements that claim to be a functional fit. This perspective is also relevant to the question of a good school: how does the school's orientation fit the economic requirements? Particularly in times of digitalisation, this is the subject of much discussion. How is it possible to create a balance between family expectations and school possibilities? Both the quantity and the quality of all-day schools play a role here. And finally, how does the school system interact with extracurricular educational institutions? This includes offerings from clubs, museums, theatres, and many more institutions. The question of a functionally appropriate school is thus an important aspect in answering the question of a good school.

The Covid-19 pandemic has now left traces in all quadrants presented: if in the objective quadrant, it is the learning deficits that may be remembered, from an interobjective point of view, it is the synergy between school and family that is important for educational success. From the perspective of the intersubjective quadrant, the question of values is on everyone's lips – solidarity is the keyword – and from the perspective of the subjective quadrant, it is joy that many have lost in the process of social isolation. In this sense, rethinking school means that all these facets of a school must be taken into account in the future so that everything is not determined by just one of the quadrants. The consequence of a one-sided view of school is an educational climate crisis because school then does not do justice to people with all their possibilities and needs. In this respect, a good school is effective, functionally appropriate, culturally appropriate, and joyful.

Averting the pedagogical climate crisis: joy becomes the leitmotif

The outlined perspectives of a good school point to an aspect that must be a wake-up call in view of a study by Lee Jenkins (2015). In this study, learners from preschool to the senior year of high school were asked to assess how much they enjoyed going to school because they enjoyed learning. The result shows that almost all learners experience joy in learning at school at the beginning of their school career. This value then slowly but surely decreases from school year to school year, until it bottoms out at a good 30 per cent in the ninth grade. Towards the end – that is, when light becomes visible at the end of the tunnel – the enjoyment of learning at school increases slightly again.

This result, also known as the Jenkins curve, is shocking. After all, the central goal of school is to maintain joy in learning and, in the process of widening the circle of thought, also to awaken a joy in learning at school. But if we now have to conclude that exactly the opposite occurs and learners feel less and less joy in learning at school as they get older, then something is going wrong in this educational institution.

What is going wrong is revealed by Ken Robinson (2018), one of the best-known educationalists of recent years, in a TED talk that is still the most-watched TED talk ever: "Do Schools Kill Creativity?" Over 70 million people have watched it. In it, Ken Robinson talks about the fact that school kills the creativity of children and young people – some school psychologists go one step further and say: school not only kills the creativity of children and young people, but it can even make them ill. As a reason for this negative finding, Ken Robinson cites a misunderstood standardisation that fails to recognise people's individuality. In addition, an understanding of mistakes that does not correspond to human learning dominates. According to this false understanding, mistakes in school are always something to be avoided. But correctly understood, errors are the motor of learning – without errors, there is no learning. And finally, he criticises a resulting superficiality that, at its core, does not do justice to human possibilities: through too much meaningless detailed knowledge, learners lose the desire to learn and thus also the joy of school.

For Ken Robinson, the consequence of the aforementioned is a "pedagogical climate crisis": children and young people grow up in a system that does not do justice to them and does not understand them. This pedagogical climate crisis is even more serious than the ecological climate crisis. Because without a climate in educational institutions that respects children and young people and gives them both time and space to develop in a comprehensive sense, children and young people cannot educate themselves comprehensively and no joy can arise. The right to light-heartedness becomes particularly clear at this point. Joy is the motor of life, education, and learning.

The crucial point now is that this educational climate crisis can be overcome just as much as the ecological climate crisis. At the beginning of the twenty-first century, we humans not only have the necessary knowledge but also the necessary opportunities. But here, too, it is time to act, on a large and small scale.

In order to be able to expand on this idea at this point, I would like to go back to the Covid-19 pandemic, because it was an exceptional situation for many young people – some researchers even speak of the greatest social experiment of mankind. Why? Due to the lockdown measures, students were torn out of their social environment several times and contacts were restricted. Due to cases of infection, some children and young people also had to be quarantined, which meant that all social contact was avoided. In total, this quickly added up to several weeks during which children and adolescents not only had to study at home but were also socially isolated.

The so-called Seneca study (cf. Zierer, 2020b) investigated the question of how learners fared after the first lockdown. The study takes its name from the Roman philosopher Seneca, who formulated criticism of schools with his saying "Non vitae, sed scholae discimus"; since then, the adaptation "Non scholae, sed vitae discimus" has served as an educational appeal. After the Covid-related school closures at the end of the last school year, a phenomenon could be observed in this context that schools have rarely, perhaps never, experienced: there was great joy on all sides that face-to-face teaching was finally taking place again. So what is it that motivates learners to go to school?

As a means of answering this question, over 2200 students from grades 7 to 12 in three German states were asked in October and November 2020 what their main motive was for going to school. Three answers had to be evaluated. The evaluation of the data results in the following picture:

In all classes, peers are in first place: 93 per cent of the learners stated that friends are the determining reason why they like to go to school. In comparison, only 72 per cent agreed with the answer that learners like to go to school because they learn something there. In view of the long time young people had to be at home, the level of agreement with the answer that learners were happy to finally get out of the home was also of interest. Only 24 per cent agreed with this.

The result shows that across all grades, peers are the most important impetus for educational processes. Against this background, the much-quoted saying, "Non scholae, sed vitae discimus", inspired by Seneca, must correctly read, "Non scholae, sed amicis discimus". We do not learn for school, but for our friends.

In this result, it is worth noting that the aforementioned approval ratings depend on the age of the learners: for example, friends, learning, and getting out of the house reach the highest level of agreement in the 7th and the 12th grade, while the lowest level is recorded in the 10th grade: going to school for learning only applies to 55 per cent in this age group. Obviously, between the ages of 15 and 16, many things are far more important than school, and school is losing importance as a place to spend time. One reason for this can be seen in the abundance of curricular content, which seems almost pointless to many students. The Seneca study thus confirms the Jenkins curve mentioned earlier, according to which the enjoyment of learning at school is high at the beginning of the school career, then drops continuously to an approval rating of a good 30 per cent, only to rise again slightly towards the end.

What does this mean for schools as the most important social institution for young people? If school is to become not only a place of learning but also an educational space and thus a place of joy, it will have to be rethought. Five aspects are characteristic of joy (cf. Zierer, 2021b): reasons, feelings, activity, success, and community. With these characteristics, the aforementioned pedagogical climate crisis can be overcome.

> School as a place of joy needs reasons: learning today often takes place without any comprehensible meaning for children and young people. Why, for example, should a high school graduate from Bavaria remember all the names of the German North Sea islands? Why are young people required to be able to name the exact number of vertebrae? And why is it significant to know how many individual books the Bible consists of? If schools cannot answer these questions, then they fail to turn learning into education. It is true that people can acquire knowledge without answers to these questions, but this knowledge will not change them as people because it does not touch them. Consequently, it has no influence on their thinking, acting, and feeling. It may be relevant for the exam, but after the exam, it will be quickly forgotten. School today must therefore not only allow the question of the meaning of learning but also make it the focus of attention.
>
> School as a place of joy needs feelings: learning today often takes place without involving the emotionality of children and young people. Knowledge is often taught as knowledge that is written in books. In class, it is rarely made clear what this knowledge has to do with the learners. Almost everyone knows the 'book-page-task game' from their school days: Open the book to page X, do task number Y – that's it in terms of educational guidance. This approach is not uncommon even today, and learners legitimately ask themselves: why should I learn this? What does this have to do with me? If learning

does not make sense to children and young people, then they are not touched by it, and emotionality is left out. But without emotionality, there can be no joy. In addition, school is increasingly reduced to learning – especially during the Covid-19 pandemic. Parties and celebrations take place at the margins of school life. The curriculum is also too full, and there is no time, it is said, if the educational climate is to be developed in the direction of joie de vivre. It is a lucky boy who has been on school trips in his school days. Today, many children in primary school have never been on a school trip, and many young people know no other trips apart from holidays with their parents. But the fact that people discover themselves on journeys and experience joy through them has been known not only since Johann Wolfgang von Goethe. For many graduates, the only memory they have is of their graduation trip, during which they often run riot in view of the misery they have experienced. School today must therefore take the emotionality of children and young people into account more than before – in both classroom and extracurricular activities.

School as a place of joy needs activity: learning today often takes place in a receiver role. Learners listen and carry out what the teacher says. This often leads to the conclusion that students are only passive. This is wrong, however, because both listening and doing are activities – and listening is one of the most important human skills. What critics are right about is the lack of design in this learning. Certainly, children and young people learn many things through imitation, and even the adult human being does this. But human beings do not stop at imitation: they try things out, modify what they have heard, look for new ways, and are creative. The word "joy of activity" sums up precisely how children and young people give free rein to their motor inventiveness while playing. Without these opportunities, students' curiosity atrophies, and so does their creativity. Learning that consists only of listening and executing does not do justice to human beings and is ultimately also inhumane. School today must therefore focus more than before on the artistic areas. Art, music, and sport belong at the centre of school because they provide creative time and space in which joy can arise.

School as a place of joy needs success: learning today often takes the form of reproducing knowledge. This is also a form of success: the teacher asks the students a question, and they give the right answer. This question-and-answer game is familiar to all of us, and sometimes it is satisfying. But for joy, more is needed. Success, in its significance for educational processes in general and for joy in particular, requires a challenge that addresses human beings in all their possibilities. Think, for example, of a concert performance that is coming up after weeks of practice. Think of a child taking its first steps and successfully tottering into the arms of its parents. Or think of a competition a team has spent a lot of time preparing for and how they get better and better from game to game until the team congeals. These are challenges of the kind described by the flow effect: starting from the level of performance, there is a fit with the task, which never challenges the person only cognitively, but always motivationally and emotionally as well. Small successes are necessary here. It is detrimental to the development of children and adolescents if they do not experience any moments of success at all and only ever fail. This is especially important in the current challenges: those who only experience the ecological crisis as a threat and have no experience of how they can do something about it themselves will possibly only experience fear and powerlessness. There is certainly no joy here. In order to cope with the current challenge, it is therefore important for children and young people to experience that they can do something, that they can act successfully. This makes, for example, the costly planting of an insect meadow, which initially has hardly any influence on the ecological climate, all the more important for the pedagogical climate. School today must therefore offer more moments of success that challenge children and young people comprehensively and appeal to them cognitively, emotionally, and motivationally.

School as a place of joy needs community: learning today often takes place as an individual achievement. This is particularly visible in examinations: the individual is always challenged. This is absurd not only in view of the fact that cooperation is necessary in all areas of later life but also in view of the importance of community for education and learning. Community is the basis for human development. This does not mean that all students have to do the same thing all the time and that the group focus should take precedence over everything else. That would be just as reductive as the exaggerated celebration of each person's individuality. Rather, a balance between the two poles is necessary: community on the one hand is just as important as individual performance on the other. The collective on the one hand can be just as educationally effective as competition on the other. As a result, the two perspectives should not be seen as opposites but as complements. In this way, one comes very close to achieving joy in school. It can be achieved, for example, through projects that originate from the lifeworld of children and young people and that are thus meaningful and emotionally appealing to them. In such projects, both perspectives work together: the performance of the individual in the group. No one manages the task of a project alone, and success is not possible without the individual. School today must therefore promote community more than before – away from the lone wolf and towards the team player.

When these processes of change are implemented in schools, schools are rethought. They change from a place of learning to an educational space. At its centre is joy, because there are conscious and diverse reasons for learning, because content is conveyed in a meaningful way and appeals to the learners emotionally, because moments of success always appeal to the whole person with all his or her possibilities, and because the community of students is not only meaningful on the playground or outside the school gates but in the classrooms. In this vision of school, the pedagogical climate crisis is overcome by means of joy, and the joy of learning at school is not successively exorcised but continually increased.

The Covid-19 pandemic has called into question, and sometimes even abolished, much of what was considered immutable in society as a whole. The education system was and is also affected. Weaknesses, some of which were already known, came into sharp focus. In terms of educational policy, however, they were repeatedly hidden and forgotten for a long time. Now an educational catastrophe is looming. The following principles form the educational framework for a master plan for preventing it. They are a kind of quintessence of the arguments presented in this book (cf. Zierer, 2021d):

1　Education, not learning: Whenever educational policy decisions are made, school must not be reduced to learning. Many things can indeed be learned in front of screens. But learning is a value-free process. For it to become education, an exchange about what has been learned is necessary – and machines cannot replace this exchange. Democracy and international understanding, but also a sense of belonging to one's homeland and sustainability, are examples of such values and are at the heart of school education. We must address these issues even or especially during the crisis. Hence the first demand: declutter the curricula so that children and young people not only learn something but also educate themselves!

2　Evidence instead of eminence: Nowhere, it seems, are there so many opinions as in the field of education. Since everyone has spent about 15,000 hours of their lives in school (cf. Rutter et al., 1980), they all have something to say about the topic – and the higher the office, the greater the eminence. But opinions are not evidence, and currently, it is not uncommon for pedagogical concerns to be overridden by virological arguments, association interests, or political motives. Educational research provides evidence in the form of comprehensible and provable statements. We should therefore pay attention to its findings, especially in times of school crisis. The second demand is therefore: establish an education council with educators of all persuasions so that children and young people have advocates for education!

3 Presence before distance: distance learning existed even before the Covid-19 pandemic, so research on it has been available for decades. The result is clear: face-to-face teaching cannot be replaced without a loss of quality. This is because education is a social process, and peers are the most important motivation for children and young people to go to school. Presence is therefore also more important than technology. The maxim of keeping schools open as long as possible is indispensable from an educational point of view. Thus, the third demand is: invest in all effective hygiene measures at schools, and please do it with a bang, so that children and young people can go to school!

4 Pedagogy before technology: Digitalisation was the big topic before Covid, and for many, it is the solution in the face of the crisis. For all the justified fascination about technology, we know after 30–40 years of educational research that technology alone will not bring about educational revolutions. Only when it is meaningfully integrated into learning environments can it become effective. Currently, there is a discussion about hybrid teaching and the opinion that it is suitable for older learners. This error in thinking is obvious and empirically proven: it is not age that is decisive for independence, but competence. A school system that has so far failed to educate learners to be self-reliant will have a hard time demanding it from them in these times of crisis. This is not to question the necessity of digital equipment in schools but to put it into perspective to the extent that only the professionalism of teachers can bring it to life. Otherwise, there is the threat of a digital media graveyard, as was recently the case with language labs and computer rooms. Therefore, the fourth demand is: digitalise the school as much as necessary but as little as possible, and always accompany corresponding investments with professionalisation measures so that children and young people can experience digital media with a recognisable added benefit!

5 Teamwork instead of lone wolves: Educational success is never a matter of the individual but always depends on several people. Parents have a central role to play. If this cooperation is reduced to zero during the crisis, then children and young people from educationally disadvantaged backgrounds will be harmed – and in the long run, so will society as a whole. Then there are schools all over the world that have managed to cope with the crisis in the best possible way from an educational standpoint. What is their secret? Not the technology. Not the location. It is the teaching staff that is led with a vision and acts as a team. In educational research, this is referred to as "collective expectation of effectiveness". This common struggle for school quality is (not

only) crucial for educational success in times of crisis. It too cannot simply be switched on, but it can be initiated at the individual school with clever, systematically coordinated, and regular short training sessions. And so the final demand is: formulate an education agenda for 2050 and ensure effective school development on the ground so that children and young people can experience school as a living space!

A lot has changed since the first lockdown, and educational policy has done a lot of its homework, especially with regard to hygiene plans and additional funds for digitalisation. As important as this is: schools are not hospitals but places of education. An educational master plan is still needed. As John F. Kennedy put it: "There is only one thing more expensive than education in the long run: no education".

References

Literature

Andresen, S. et al. (2020): "Die Corona-Pandemie hat mir wertvolle Zeit genommen", Jugendalltag 2020, Universitätsverlag Hildesheim.

Barmer (2021): BARMER Arztreport 2021. https://www.barmer.de/blob/282916/0 43d9a7bf773a8810548d18dec661895/data/barmer-arztreport-2021.pdf

Betthäuser, B. A., Bach-Mortensen, A. M. & Engzell, P. (2023): A systematic review and meta-analysis of the evidence on learning during the COVID-19 pandemic. Nature Human Behaviour. https://doi.org/10.1038/s41562-022-01506-4

Bignardi, G. et al. (2020): Longitudinal increases in childhood depression symptoms during the COVID-19 lockdown. Archives of Disease in Childhood, 0, S. 1–7. https://doi.org/10.1136/archdischild-2020-320372

BKA (2019): Partnerschaftsgewalt. Kriminalstatistische Auswertung – Berichtsjahr 2019, Wiesbaden.

Boum, Samuel Simon (2003): Die Lernwirksamkeit des Schulfernsehens und seine mögliche Rolle im Bildungssystem von Kamerun. Dissertation. Hamburg.

Brophy, J. E. (1999): Teaching, Genf.

Buber, M. (1958): Ich und Du, Heidelberg.

Csíkszentmihályi, M. (2010): Das flow-Erlebnis, Stuttgart.

Dahrendorf, R. (1965): Bildung ist Bürgerrecht. Hamburg.

DAK (2021): DAK Psychreport 2021. https://www.dak.de/dak/download/report-2429408.pdf

Damerow, S. et al. (2020): Die gesundheitliche Lage in Deutschland in der Anfangsphase der COVID-19-Pandemie. Zeitliche Entwicklung ausgewählter Indikatoren der Studie GEDA 2019/2020-EHIS. Journal of Health Monitoring, 5(4). DOI:https://doi.org/10.25646/7171

Deci, E. L. et al. (1993): Die Selbstbestimmungstheorie der Motivation und ihre Bedeutung für die Pädagogik. Zeitschrift für Pädagogik, 39(2), S. 223–238.

DPtV (2021): Patientenanfragen während der Corona-Pandemie. https://www.deutschepsychotherapeutenvereinigung.de/index.php?eID=dumpFile&t=f&f=1 1802&token=68422b9d5fec27bb7944192837a7dc5d8b5a0292

Ebbinghaus, H. (1885): Über das Gedächtnis. Untersuchungen zur experimentellen Psychologie. Leipzig.

Eickelmann, B. et al. (2019): ICILS 2018 #Deutschland. Computer- und informations-bezogene Kompetenzen von SchÜlerinnen und SchÜlern im zweiten internation-alen Vergleich und Kompetenzen im Bereich Computational Thinking. MÜnster.

Erikson, E. H. (1966): Identität und Lebenszyklus, Frankfurt.

Fegert, J. M. et al. (2020): Challenges and burden of the Coronavirus 2019 (CO-VID-19) pandemic for child and adolescent mental health: a narrative review to highlight clinical and research needs in the acute phase and the long return to normality. Child Adolesc Psychiatry Ment Health, 14, 20. https://doi.org/10.1186/s13034-020-00329-3

Gardner, H. (1983): Frames of Mind – The Theory of Multiple Intelligences, Basic Books.

Gardner, H. (2009): Five Minds for the Future, Harvard.

Habermas, J. (2019): Auch eine kleine Geschichte der Philosophie, Frankfurt.

Hamilton, E. R. et al. (2016): The substitution augmentation modification redefini-tion (SAMR) model: a critical review and suggestions for its use. TechTrends, 60, S. 433–441. https://doi.org/10.1007/s11528-016-0091-y

Hattie, J. (2015): What doesn't work in education: the politics of distraction. Open Ideas at Pearson. https://www.pearson.com/hattie/distractions.html

Hattie, J. et al. (2019): Visible Learning Insights. London.

Helmke, A. (2014): Unterrichtsqualität und Lehrerprofessionalität. Diagnose, Evaluation und Verbesserung des Unterrichts. Stuttgart.

Hentig, H. V. (2003): Die Schule neu denken. Eine Übung in pädagogischer Ver-nunft, Weinheim u. a.

Jenkins, L. (2015): Optimize Your School. Thousand Oaks.

Klafki, W. (1995): Neue Studien zur Bildungstheorie. Zeitgemäße Allgemeinbil-dung und kritisch-konstruktive Didaktik, Weinheim.

Koletzko, B. et al. (2021): Lifestyle and body weight consequences of the CO-VID-19 pandemic in children: increasing disparity. Annals in Nutrition and Me-tabolism. https://doi.org/10.1159/000514186

König, C. et al. (2022): The impact of COVID-19-related school closures on stu-dent achievement—a meta-analysis. Educational Measurement, https://doi.org/10.1111/emip.12495

López-Bueno, R. et al. (2021): Potential health-related behaviors for pre-school and school-aged children during COVID-19 lockdown: a narrative review. Pre-ventive Medicine, 143, 106349.

Luhmann, N. (1998): Die Gesellschaft der Gesellschaft, Frankfurt.

MET (2010): Learning about Teaching, Bill & Melinda Gates Foundation.

Meyer, H. (2004): Was ist guter Unterricht? Mit didaktischer Landkarte, Berlin.

Molnár, G. et al. (2023): Short- and long-term effects of COVID-related kindergar-ten and school closures on first- to eighth-grade students' school readiness skills and mathematics, reading and science learning. Learning and Instruction, 83. https://doi.org/10.1016/j.learninstruc.2022.101706

mpfs (Medienpädagogischer Forschungsverbund SÜdwest) (2020): JIM 2019: Ju-gend, Information, Medien, Basisuntersuchung zum Medienumgang 12- bis 19-Jähriger in Deutschland, Stuttgart.

Nida-Rümelin, J. (2011): Die Optimierungsfalle: Philosophie einer humanen Öko-nomie, München.

Nida-Rümelin, J. et al. (2018): Entrümpelt die Lehrpläne, in: SPIEGEL, Nr. 27.

Nida-Rümelin, J. et al. (2020): Die Debatte über digitale Bildung ist entgleist. Neue Zürcher Zeitung, S. 8.

Nowossadeck, S. et al. (2021): Körperliche Aktivität in der Corona- Pandemie: Veränderung der Häufigkeit von Sport und Spazierengehen bei Menschen in der zweiten Lebenshälfte, DZA Aktuell, Berlin.

Panda, P. K. et al. (2021): Psychological and behavioral impact of lockdown and quarantine measures for COVID-19 pandemic on children, adolescents and caregivers: a systematic review and meta-analysis. Journal of Tropical Pediatrics, 67(1), fmaa122. https://doi.org/10.1093/tropej/fmaa122

Picht, G. (1964): Die deutsche Bildungskatastrophe, Freiburg im Breisgau.

Puentedura, R. R. (2021): SAMR: a brief introduction, http://hippasus.com/rrpweblog/archives/2015/10/SAMR_ABriefIntro.pdf

Ravens-Sieberer, U. et al. (2021): Seelische Gesundheit und psychische Belastungen von Kindern und Jugendlichen in der ersten Welle der COVID-19- Pandemie – Ergebnisse der COPSY-Studie. Bundesgesundheitsblatt, 2021. https://doi.org/10.1007/s00103-021-03291-3

Ricking, H. et al. (2016): Schulabsentismus und Schulabbruch, Stuttgart.

Robinson, K. (2018): You, Your Child, and School: Navigate Your Way to the Best Education, Viking.

Röhr, S. et al. (2020): Psychosoziale Folgen von Quarantänemaßnahmen bei schwerwiegenden Coronavirus-AusbrÜchen: ein Rapid Review. Psychiat Prax, 47, S. 179–189.

Rutter, M. et al. (1980): 15 000 Stunden. Schulen und ihre Wirkung auf die Kinder, Weilheim.

Schlack, R. et al. (2020): Auswirkungen der COVID-19-Pandemie und der Eindämmungs- maßnahmen auf die psychische Gesundheit von Kindern und Jugendlichen. Journal of Health Monitoring, 5(4), S. 23–34.

Schmidt, S. C. E. et al. (2020): Physical activity and screen time of children and adolescents before and during the COVID-19 lockdown in Germany: a natural experiment. Nature Scientific Report, 10(1), 21780. https://doi.org/10.1038/s41598-020-78438-4

Sennet, R. (2014): Zusammenarbeit: Was unsere Gesellschaft zusammenhält, MÜnchen.

Steinert, C. et al. (2020): Gewalt an Frauen und Kindern in Deutschland während COVID-19-bedingten Ausgangsbeschränkungen: Zusammenfassung der Ergebnisse. https://celleheute.de/sites/default/files/dokumente/2020-11/Zusammen fassung%20der%20Studienergebnisse.pdf

Unger, V. et al. (2020): Unterricht während der Corona-Pandemie. PFLB, 2(6), 84–99. https://doi.org/10.4119/pflb-3907

Wang, J. et al. (2021): Progression of myopia in school-aged children after CO-VID-19 home confinement. JAMA Ophthalmology, 139(3), 293–300. https://doi.org/10.1001/jamaophthalmol.2020.6239

Wilber, K. (1987): Das Wahre, Schöne, Gute, Frankfurt.

Wößmann, L. et al. (2020): Bildung in der Coronakrise: Wie haben die Schulkinder die Zeit der Schulschließungen verbracht, und welche Bildungsmaßnahmen befÜrworten die Deutschen?, ifo Schnelldienst, 9, München.

Wu, P.-C. et al. (2018): Myopia prevention in Taiwan. Annals of Eye Science, 2018, 3, 12. https://doi.org/10.1016/j.ophtha.2017.12.011

Zierer, K. (2019): Putting learning before technology! In: The Possibilities and Limits of Digitalization, London.

Zierer, K. (2020a): FÜr Junge ist der schulische Lockdown eine so- ziale Katastrophe – der Schutz der Gesellschaft darf nicht un- verhältnismässig auf ihre Kosten gehen. NZZ, 24(11).

Zierer, K. (2020b): Für die Freunde lernen wir! In: DIE ZEIT, Nr. 54

Zierer, K. (2020c): Herausforderung Homeschooling, Baltmannsweiler.

Zierer, K. (2021a): Hattie für gestresste Lehrer 2.0, Baltmannsweiler.

Zierer, K. (2021b): Prinzip Freude, München.

Zierer, K. (2021c): Effects of pandemic-related school closures on pupils' performance and learning in selected countries: a rapid review. Education Sciences, 11(6), 252. doi.org/10.3390/educsci11060252

Zierer, K. (2021d): Schulen sind keine Krankenhäuser. In: FOCUS, Nr. 3.

Zierer, K. (2021e): Das Herz der Lehrerbildung. Bayerische Schule, Heft 1, S. 21–25.

Index

Printed in the United States
by Baker & Taylor Publisher Services